ROAD TRIP BIN×G

A TOWN WATER TOWER IS PAINTED TO LOOK LIKE SOMETHING KITSCHY.	BATHROOMS AT THE GAS STATION ARE TOO GROSS TO USE.	A CAR HAS WILDLY EXPIRED TEMPORARY TAGS.	A ROADSIDE 'ATTRACTION' LOOKS LIKE IT'S BEEN CLOSED FOR 100 YEARS.	THERE'S A MOTORCYCLE THAT'S THE SIZE OF A SMALL CAR.
SOMEONE IS WALKING ON THE SIDE OF THE HIGHWAY.	A LANE IS CLOSED FOR REPAIRS—THAT NO ONE IS ACTUALLY WORKING ON.	THE PHRASE 'ARE WE THERE YET?' IS UTTERED.	AN OLD SCHOOL BUS HAS BEEN CONVERTED INTO AN RV.	A ROADSIDE BILLBOARD ADVERTISES THE WORLD'S BEST FUDGE.
'CLEAN ME' IS WRITTEN IN DIRT ON A PASSING VEHICLE.	THE RADIO STATION JUST TURNS INTO STATIC.	✖	A TRUCK STOP HAS ITS OWN EATING CHALLENGE FOR A FREE T-SHIRT.	A VEHICLE PLASTERED IN NONSENSICAL BUMPER STICKERS IS SPOTTED.
A LIVESTOCK TRAILER IS SMELLED BEFORE IT IS SEEN.	EVERYONE SUDDENLY STARTS GOING THE SPEED LIMIT BECAUSE OF A COP.	MALE GENITALIA IS FEATURED AS 'DECOR' ON THE BACK OF A TRUCK.	'ON THE ROAD AGAIN' IS SAID/SUNG AFTER A PIT STOP.	SOMEONE IS GOING 20 MILES UNDER THE SPEED LIMIT IN THE FAST LANE.
AN OPEN-BED TRUCK HAS A DOG AND/OR CHILD RIDING IN THE BACK.	AN 'ADULT SUPERSTORE' IS LOCATED RIGHT BESIDE A FIREWORKS SHOP.	A MINIVAN HAS THEMED STICKERS REPRESENTING AN ENORMOUS FAMILY.	ANOTHER CAR'S BLINKER IS LEFT ON FOR MILES.	A CAR USING A TINY SPARE TIRE PASSES YOU AT 85 MPH.

OBJECTIVE

OH, YOU MEAN BESIDES TRYING TO PASS THE TIME DURING THIS VACATION THAT YOU MAY OR MAY NOT HAVE EVEN WANTED TO GO ON? ISN'T THAT ENOUGH? WHAT DO YOU WANT FROM US?

WELL, WE HOPE YOU'RE AT LEAST FAMILIAR WITH THE CONCEPT OF BINGO. BECAUSE IF NOT, WELL WE ARE REALLY KIND OF WORRIED ABOUT YOU. WHAT OTHER THINGS IN LIFE HAVE YOU MISSED? SHOES? AUTOMOBILES? TWO-PLY TOILET PAPER? WE DIGRESS.

THIS VACATION BIN·GO GAME IS PLAYED MUCH LIKE THE TRADITIONAL ONE. YOUR GOAL IS TO SIMPLY BE THE FIRST TO FILL 5 SEQUENTIAL SQUARES IN A ROW, A COLUMN, OR EVEN DIAGONALLY (SEE FIGURE 1 BELOW).

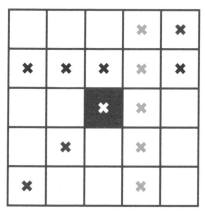

FIGURE 1

SEE THAT X IN THE CENTER SQUARE OF YOUR BOARDS? THAT'S A FREE SQUARE—WHICH MEANS EVERY PLAYER GETS THIS ONE AUTOMATICALLY. IT REALLY HELPS SO...YOU'RE WELCOME.

PLAYING THE GAME

AFTER DETERMINING HOW MANY PEOPLE ARE PLAYING, THE OWNER OF THE BOOK SHOULD PERF. OUT A CARD (OR TWO) FOR EVERYONE TO USE AS THEIR PLAY BOARD(S).

ALRIGHT, SO HERE'S HOW OUR GAME IS A BIT DIFFERENT. WE'VE PRE-FILLED EACH CARD WITH THE COMMON (YET RIDICULOUS) THINGS THAT ALWAYS SEEM TO HAPPEN WHILE TRAVELING. SO, INSTEAD OF SOMEONE JUST CALLING OUT NUMBERS, EVERYONE IS PEOPLE WATCHING INSTEAD. WHEN SOMETHING HAPPENS THAT IS ON ONE OF YOUR SQUARES, YOU CALL IT OUT (AS DISCREETLY AS APPROPRIATE, OF COURSE) AND MARK OFF THE SQUARE.

JUST REMEMBER THAT THE OTHER PLAYERS NEED TO BE AWARE OF THE 'CALL'—AND IDEALLY SEE IT AS WELL (BUT THAT'S NOT A REQUIREMENT). THAT WAY THEY CAN ALSO MARK OFF THAT SQUARE IF IT'S ON THEIR BOARD.

WINNING

WHEN A PLAYER MARKS OFF A WINNING CARD, THEY SHOULD ANNOUNCE 'BINGO.' IN THE EVENT OF A TIE, THE FIRST TO SAY IT IS THE WINNER. EITHER WAY—EVERYONE ELSE IN THE ROOM WILL PROBABLY BE WONDERING WHAT THE HELL YOU ARE DOING. ADMITTEDLY IT MIGHT BE HARD TO MAKE A TRUE BINGO, SO YOU CAN ALSO DECIDE THAT THE PLAYER WITH THE MOST SQUARES MARKED OFF IS THE WINNER.

BONUS: YOU CAN ALSO PLAY THIS AS A DRINKING GAME. IT'S SIMPLE. WHEN SOMETHING HAPPENS ON YOUR CARD, YOU HAVE TO TAKE A DRINK (AFTER TRAVELING IS DONE OF COURSE). IF YOU MAKE A BINGO—WELL NOW EVERYONE ELSE HAS TO DRINK. JUST TALLY UP DRINKS ONCE YOU'RE AT YOUR DESTINATION & GO TO THE BAR.

THERE'S A CAR WITH A SET OF EYELASHES ON THE HEADLIGHTS.	A ROADSIDE FRUIT STAND IS SELLING QUESTIONABLE PRODUCE.	A DIGITAL ROAD SIGN DISPLAYS A 'JOKE' ABOUT TRAFFIC SAFETY.	SOMEONE AT THE GAS STATION IS LITERALLY WEARING PAJAMAS.	THERE'S A QUIRKY BILLBOARD FOR A PREDATORY LAWYER.
THERE'S A CASINO INSIDE OF A GAS STATION.	A STATE REST STOP IS USED WITHOUT EVEN BEING MURDERED.	THERE'S A WESTERN WEAR STORE—NOT EVEN CLOSE TO THE ACTUAL WEST.	A PASSENGER HAS THEIR BARE FEET ON THE DASHBOARD OF A CAR.	A BUNCH OF OLD TIMEY CARS APPEAR OUT OF NOWHERE ON THE HIGHWAY.
AN ACTUAL TUMBLEWEED BLOWS ACROSS THE ROAD.	GAS STATION HOT DOGS APPEAR TO HAVE BEEN ON THE ROLLERS SINCE 2012.	✖	AN ACTUAL HITCHHIKER IS SEEN—DESPITE IT NOT BEING 1974.	A CONFUSING PERSONALIZED LICENSE PLATE IS SPOTTED.
THERE'S AN OVER-SIZED LOAD HAULING MYSTERY EQUIPMENT AT 35 MPH.	SOMEONE IS HAULING A BROKEN DOWN COUCH THAT ISN'T EVEN TIED DOWN.	A SLOW CAR STARTS TO SPEED UP THE MOMENT THAT SOMEONE TRIES TO PASS.	A HOMEMADE BILLBOARD SPICES UP THE LANDSCAPE OF A LOCAL CORNFIELD.	A CAR IS SO PACKED FULL OF JUNK THAT ALL OF THE WINDOWS ARE BLOCKED.
A TOWN CONSISTS OF A DINER AND A GAS STATION—THAT BOTH CLOSE AT 6.	THERE'S A NON-PIZZA BUSINESS OPERATING IN AN OLD PIZZA HUT.	AN 80 YEAR-OLD MAN IS DRIVING AN RV BIGGER THAN MOST HOUSES.	A MOTEL ADVERTISES THAT IT HAS COLOR TELEVISION.	SOMEONE IS 'DRIVING' A HORSE AND BUGGY ON THE HIGHWAY.

OBJECTIVE

OH, YOU MEAN BESIDES TRYING TO PASS THE TIME DURING THIS VACATION THAT YOU MAY OR MAY NOT HAVE EVEN WANTED TO GO ON? ISN'T THAT ENOUGH? WHAT DO YOU WANT FROM US?

WELL, WE HOPE YOU'RE AT LEAST FAMILIAR WITH THE CONCEPT OF BINGO. BECAUSE IF NOT, WELL WE ARE REALLY KIND OF WORRIED ABOUT YOU. WHAT OTHER THINGS IN LIFE HAVE YOU MISSED? SHOES? AUTOMOBILES? TWO-PLY TOILET PAPER? WE DIGRESS.

THIS VACATION BIN·GO GAME IS PLAYED MUCH LIKE THE TRADITIONAL ONE. YOUR GOAL IS TO SIMPLY BE THE FIRST TO FILL 5 SEQUENTIAL SQUARES IN A ROW, A COLUMN, OR EVEN DIAGONALLY (SEE FIGURE 1 BELOW).

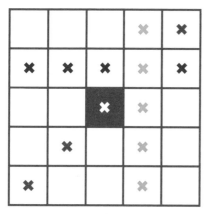

FIGURE 1

SEE THAT X IN THE CENTER SQUARE OF YOUR BOARDS? THAT'S A FREE SQUARE—WHICH MEANS EVERY PLAYER GETS THIS ONE AUTOMATICALLY. IT REALLY HELPS SO...YOU'RE WELCOME.

PLAYING THE GAME

AFTER DETERMINING HOW MANY PEOPLE ARE PLAYING, THE OWNER OF THE BOOK SHOULD PERF. OUT A CARD (OR TWO) FOR EVERYONE TO USE AS THEIR PLAY BOARD(S).

ALRIGHT, SO HERE'S HOW OUR GAME IS A BIT DIFFERENT. WE'VE PRE-FILLED EACH CARD WITH THE COMMON (YET RIDICULOUS) THINGS THAT ALWAYS SEEM TO HAPPEN WHILE TRAVELING. SO, INSTEAD OF SOMEONE JUST CALLING OUT NUMBERS, EVERYONE IS PEOPLE WATCHING INSTEAD. WHEN SOMETHING HAPPENS THAT IS ON ONE OF YOUR SQUARES, YOU CALL IT OUT (AS DISCREETLY AS APPROPRIATE, OF COURSE) AND MARK OFF THE SQUARE.

JUST REMEMBER THAT THE OTHER PLAYERS NEED TO BE AWARE OF THE 'CALL'—AND IDEALLY SEE IT AS WELL (BUT THAT'S NOT A REQUIREMENT). THAT WAY THEY CAN ALSO MARK OFF THAT SQUARE IF IT'S ON THEIR BOARD.

WINNING

WHEN A PLAYER MARKS OFF A WINNING CARD, THEY SHOULD ANNOUNCE 'BINGO.' IN THE EVENT OF A TIE, THE FIRST TO SAY IT IS THE WINNER. EITHER WAY—EVERYONE ELSE IN THE ROOM WILL PROBABLY BE WONDERING WHAT THE HELL YOU ARE DOING. ADMITTEDLY IT MIGHT BE HARD TO MAKE A TRUE BINGO, SO YOU CAN ALSO DECIDE THAT THE PLAYER WITH THE MOST SQUARES MARKED OFF IS THE WINNER.

BONUS: YOU CAN ALSO PLAY THIS AS A DRINKING GAME. IT'S SIMPLE. WHEN SOMETHING HAPPENS ON YOUR CARD, YOU HAVE TO TAKE A DRINK (AFTER TRAVELING IS DONE OF COURSE). IF YOU MAKE A BINGO—WELL NOW EVERYONE ELSE HAS TO DRINK. JUST TALLY UP DRINKS ONCE YOU'RE AT YOUR DESTINATION & GO TO THE BAR.

ROAD TRIP BIN×GO ROAD TRIP

A CAR IS SO PACKED FULL OF JUNK THAT ALL OF THE WINDOWS ARE BLOCKED.	A DIGITAL ROAD SIGN DISPLAYS A 'JOKE' ABOUT TRAFFIC SAFETY.	THE RADIO STATION JUST TURNS INTO STATIC.	GAS STATION HOT DOGS APPEAR TO HAVE BEEN ON THE ROLLERS SINCE 2012.	SOMEONE IS WALKING ON THE SIDE OF THE HIGHWAY.
THERE'S A CASINO INSIDE OF A GAS STATION.	'ON THE ROAD AGAIN' IS SAID/SUNG AFTER A PIT STOP.	SOMEONE IS HAULING A BROKEN DOWN COUCH THAT ISN'T EVEN TIED DOWN.	A TRUCK STOP HAS ITS OWN EATING CHALLENGE FOR A FREE T-SHIRT.	EVERYONE SUDDENLY STARTS GOING THE SPEED LIMIT BECAUSE OF A COP.
A CONFUSING PERSONALIZED LICENSE PLATE IS SPOTTED.	A LIVESTOCK TRAILER IS SMELLED BEFORE IT IS SEEN.	✖	THERE'S AN OVER-SIZED LOAD HAULING MYSTERY EQUIPMENT AT 35 MPH.	SOMEONE IS 'DRIVING' A HORSE AND BUGGY ON THE HIGHWAY.
A SLOW CAR STARTS TO SPEED UP THE MOMENT THAT SOMEONE TRIES TO PASS.	SOMEONE AT THE GAS STATION IS LITERALLY WEARING PAJAMAS.	THERE'S A QUIRKY BILLBOARD FOR A PREDATORY LAWYER.	A MOTEL ADVERTISES THAT IT HAS COLOR TELEVISION.	A STATE REST STOP IS USED WITHOUT EVEN BEING MURDERED.
A VEHICLE PLASTERED IN NONSENSICAL BUMPER STICKERS IS SPOTTED.	MALE GENITALIA IS FEATURED AS 'DECOR' ON THE BACK OF A TRUCK.	THERE'S A NON-PIZZA BUSINESS OPERATING IN AN OLD PIZZA HUT.	A ROADSIDE FRUIT STAND IS SELLING QUESTIONABLE PRODUCE.	A PASSENGER HAS THEIR BARE FEET ON THE DASHBOARD OF A CAR.

OBJECTIVE

OH, YOU MEAN BESIDES TRYING TO PASS THE TIME DURING THIS VACATION THAT YOU MAY OR MAY NOT HAVE EVEN WANTED TO GO ON? ISN'T THAT ENOUGH? WHAT DO YOU WANT FROM US?

WELL, WE HOPE YOU'RE AT LEAST FAMILIAR WITH THE CONCEPT OF BINGO. BECAUSE IF NOT, WELL WE ARE REALLY KIND OF WORRIED ABOUT YOU. WHAT OTHER THINGS IN LIFE HAVE YOU MISSED? SHOES? AUTOMOBILES? TWO-PLY TOILET PAPER? WE DIGRESS.

THIS VACATION BIN·GO GAME IS PLAYED MUCH LIKE THE TRADITIONAL ONE. YOUR GOAL IS TO SIMPLY BE THE FIRST TO FILL 5 SEQUENTIAL SQUARES IN A ROW, A COLUMN, OR EVEN DIAGONALLY (SEE FIGURE 1 BELOW).

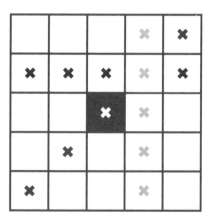

FIGURE 1

SEE THAT X IN THE CENTER SQUARE OF YOUR BOARDS? THAT'S A FREE SQUARE—WHICH MEANS EVERY PLAYER GETS THIS ONE AUTOMATICALLY. IT REALLY HELPS SO...YOU'RE WELCOME.

PLAYING THE GAME

AFTER DETERMINING HOW MANY PEOPLE ARE PLAYING, THE OWNER OF THE BOOK SHOULD PERF. OUT A CARD (OR TWO) FOR EVERYONE TO USE AS THEIR PLAY BOARD(S).

ALRIGHT, SO HERE'S HOW OUR GAME IS A BIT DIFFERENT. WE'VE PRE-FILLED EACH CARD WITH THE COMMON (YET RIDICULOUS) THINGS THAT ALWAYS SEEM TO HAPPEN WHILE TRAVELING. SO, INSTEAD OF SOMEONE JUST CALLING OUT NUMBERS, EVERYONE IS PEOPLE WATCHING INSTEAD. WHEN SOMETHING HAPPENS THAT IS ON ONE OF YOUR SQUARES, YOU CALL IT OUT (AS DISCREETLY AS APPROPRIATE, OF COURSE) AND MARK OFF THE SQUARE.

JUST REMEMBER THAT THE OTHER PLAYERS NEED TO BE AWARE OF THE 'CALL'—AND IDEALLY SEE IT AS WELL (BUT THAT'S NOT A REQUIREMENT). THAT WAY THEY CAN ALSO MARK OFF THAT SQUARE IF IT'S ON THEIR BOARD.

WINNING

WHEN A PLAYER MARKS OFF A WINNING CARD, THEY SHOULD ANNOUNCE 'BINGO.' IN THE EVENT OF A TIE, THE FIRST TO SAY IT IS THE WINNER. EITHER WAY—EVERYONE ELSE IN THE ROOM WILL PROBABLY BE WONDERING WHAT THE HELL YOU ARE DOING. ADMITTEDLY IT MIGHT BE HARD TO MAKE A TRUE BINGO, SO YOU CAN ALSO DECIDE THAT THE PLAYER WITH THE MOST SQUARES MARKED OFF IS THE WINNER.

BONUS: YOU CAN ALSO PLAY THIS AS A DRINKING GAME. IT'S SIMPLE. WHEN SOMETHING HAPPENS ON YOUR CARD, YOU HAVE TO TAKE A DRINK (AFTER TRAVELING IS DONE OF COURSE). IF YOU MAKE A BINGO—WELL NOW EVERYONE ELSE HAS TO DRINK. JUST TALLY UP DRINKS ONCE YOU'RE AT YOUR DESTINATION & GO TO THE BAR.

ROAD TRIP BIN×GO ROAD TRIP

SOMEONE IS 'DRIVING' A HORSE AND BUGGY ON THE HIGHWAY.	BATHROOMS AT THE GAS STATION ARE TOO GROSS TO USE.	AN OPEN-BED TRUCK HAS A DOG AND/OR CHILD RIDING IN THE BACK.	ANOTHER CAR'S BLINKER IS LEFT ON FOR MILES.	A SLOW CAR STARTS TO SPEED UP THE MOMENT THAT SOMEONE TRIES TO PASS.
AN 80 YEAR-OLD MAN IS DRIVING AN RV BIGGER THAN MOST HOUSES.	A CAR IS SO PACKED FULL OF JUNK THAT ALL OF THE WINDOWS ARE BLOCKED.	'CLEAN ME' IS WRITTEN IN DIRT ON A PASSING VEHICLE.	AN OLD SCHOOL BUS HAS BEEN CONVERTED INTO AN RV.	A PASSENGER HAS THEIR BARE FEET ON THE DASHBOARD OF A CAR.
A CONFUSING PERSONALIZED LICENSE PLATE IS SPOTTED.	MALE GENITALIA IS FEATURED AS 'DECOR' ON THE BACK OF A TRUCK.	✖	THERE'S A CAR WITH A SET OF EYELASHES ON THE HEADLIGHTS.	A MINIVAN HAS THEMED STICKERS REPRESENTING AN ENORMOUS FAMILY.
A STATE REST STOP IS USED WITHOUT EVEN BEING MURDERED.	SOMEONE IS WALKING ON THE SIDE OF THE HIGHWAY.	THERE'S A MOTORCYCLE THAT'S THE SIZE OF A SMALL CAR.	A HOMEMADE BILLBOARD SPICES UP THE LANDSCAPE OF A LOCAL CORNFIELD.	A MOTEL ADVERTISES THAT IT HAS COLOR TELEVISION.
THERE'S A CASINO INSIDE OF A GAS STATION.	AN 'ADULT SUPERSTORE' IS LOCATED RIGHT BESIDE A FIREWORKS SHOP.	A TOWN CONSISTS OF A DINER AND A GAS STATION—THAT BOTH CLOSE AT 6.	A ROADSIDE BILLBOARD ADVERTISES THE WORLD'S BEST FUDGE.	EVERYONE SUDDENLY STARTS GOING THE SPEED LIMIT BECAUSE OF A COP.

OBJECTIVE

OH, YOU MEAN BESIDES TRYING TO PASS THE TIME DURING THIS VACATION THAT YOU MAY OR MAY NOT HAVE EVEN WANTED TO GO ON? ISN'T THAT ENOUGH? WHAT DO YOU WANT FROM US?

WELL, WE HOPE YOU'RE AT LEAST FAMILIAR WITH THE CONCEPT OF BINGO. BECAUSE IF NOT, WELL WE ARE REALLY KIND OF WORRIED ABOUT YOU. WHAT OTHER THINGS IN LIFE HAVE YOU MISSED? SHOES? AUTOMOBILES? TWO-PLY TOILET PAPER? WE DIGRESS.

THIS VACATION BIN×GO GAME IS PLAYED MUCH LIKE THE TRADITIONAL ONE. YOUR GOAL IS TO SIMPLY BE THE FIRST TO FILL 5 SEQUENTIAL SQUARES IN A ROW, A COLUMN, OR EVEN DIAGONALLY (SEE FIGURE 1 BELOW).

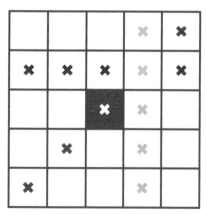

FIGURE 1

SEE THAT X IN THE CENTER SQUARE OF YOUR BOARDS? THAT'S A FREE SQUARE—WHICH MEANS EVERY PLAYER GETS THIS ONE AUTOMATICALLY. IT REALLY HELPS SO...YOU'RE WELCOME.

PLAYING THE GAME

AFTER DETERMINING HOW MANY PEOPLE ARE PLAYING, THE OWNER OF THE BOOK SHOULD PERF. OUT A CARD (OR TWO) FOR EVERYONE TO USE AS THEIR PLAY BOARD(S).

ALRIGHT, SO HERE'S HOW OUR GAME IS A BIT DIFFERENT. WE'VE PRE-FILLED EACH CARD WITH THE COMMON (YET RIDICULOUS) THINGS THAT ALWAYS SEEM TO HAPPEN WHILE TRAVELING. SO, INSTEAD OF SOMEONE JUST CALLING OUT NUMBERS, EVERYONE IS PEOPLE WATCHING INSTEAD. WHEN SOMETHING HAPPENS THAT IS ON ONE OF YOUR SQUARES, YOU CALL IT OUT (AS DISCREETLY AS APPROPRIATE, OF COURSE) AND MARK OFF THE SQUARE.

JUST REMEMBER THAT THE OTHER PLAYERS NEED TO BE AWARE OF THE 'CALL'—AND IDEALLY SEE IT AS WELL (BUT THAT'S NOT A REQUIREMENT). THAT WAY THEY CAN ALSO MARK OFF THAT SQUARE IF IT'S ON THEIR BOARD.

WINNING

WHEN A PLAYER MARKS OFF A WINNING CARD, THEY SHOULD ANNOUNCE 'BINGO.' IN THE EVENT OF A TIE, THE FIRST TO SAY IT IS THE WINNER. EITHER WAY—EVERYONE ELSE IN THE ROOM WILL PROBABLY BE WONDERING WHAT THE HELL YOU ARE DOING. ADMITTEDLY IT MIGHT BE HARD TO MAKE A TRUE BINGO, SO YOU CAN ALSO DECIDE THAT THE PLAYER WITH THE MOST SQUARES MARKED OFF IS THE WINNER.

BONUS: YOU CAN ALSO PLAY THIS AS A DRINKING GAME. IT'S SIMPLE. WHEN SOMETHING HAPPENS ON YOUR CARD, YOU HAVE TO TAKE A DRINK (AFTER TRAVELING IS DONE OF COURSE). IF YOU MAKE A BINGO—WELL NOW EVERYONE ELSE HAS TO DRINK. JUST TALLY UP DRINKS ONCE YOU'RE AT YOUR DESTINATION & GO TO THE BAR.

A HOMEMADE BILLBOARD SPICES UP THE LANDSCAPE OF A LOCAL CORNFIELD.	A LIVESTOCK TRAILER IS SMELLED BEFORE IT IS SEEN.	A VEHICLE PLASTERED IN NONSENSICAL BUMPER STICKERS IS SPOTTED.	THERE'S AN OVER-SIZED LOAD HAULING MYSTERY EQUIPMENT AT 35 MPH.	'ON THE ROAD AGAIN' IS SAID/SUNG AFTER A PIT STOP.
A LANE IS CLOSED FOR REPAIRS—THAT NO ONE IS ACTUALLY WORKING ON.	A BUNCH OF OLD-TIMEY CARS APPEAR OUT OF NOWHERE ON THE HIGHWAY.	SOMEONE IS GOING 20 MILES UNDER THE SPEED LIMIT IN THE FAST LANE.	A TRUCK STOP HAS ITS OWN EATING CHALLENGE FOR A FREE T-SHIRT.	SOMEONE IS WALKING ON THE SIDE OF THE HIGHWAY.
A ROADSIDE 'ATTRACTION' LOOKS LIKE IT'S BEEN CLOSED FOR 100 YEARS.	AN ACTUAL HITCHHIKER IS SEEN—DESPITE IT NOT BEING 1974.	✖	BATHROOMS AT THE GAS STATION ARE TOO GROSS TO USE.	AN OPEN-BED TRUCK HAS A DOG AND/OR CHILD RIDING IN THE BACK.
THE RADIO STATION JUST TURNS INTO STATIC.	A TOWN WATER TOWER IS PAINTED TO LOOK LIKE SOMETHING KITSCHY.	AN 80 YEAR-OLD MAN IS DRIVING AN RV BIGGER THAN MOST HOUSES.	THERE'S A CASINO INSIDE OF A GAS STATION.	A MINIVAN HAS THEMED STICKERS REPRESENTING AN ENORMOUS FAMILY.
THERE'S A NON-PIZZA BUSINESS OPERATING IN AN OLD PIZZA HUT.	A CAR USING A TINY SPARE TIRE PASSES YOU AT 85 MPH.	AN ACTUAL TUMBLEWEED BLOWS ACROSS THE ROAD.	A DIGITAL ROAD SIGN DISPLAYS A 'JOKE' ABOUT TRAFFIC SAFETY.	THERE'S A WESTERN WEAR STORE—NOT EVEN CLOSE TO THE ACTUAL WEST.

OBJECTIVE

OH, YOU MEAN BESIDES TRYING TO PASS THE TIME DURING THIS VACATION THAT YOU MAY OR MAY NOT HAVE EVEN WANTED TO GO ON? ISN'T THAT ENOUGH? WHAT DO YOU WANT FROM US?

WELL, WE HOPE YOU'RE AT LEAST FAMILIAR WITH THE CONCEPT OF BINGO. BECAUSE IF NOT, WELL WE ARE REALLY KIND OF WORRIED ABOUT YOU. WHAT OTHER THINGS IN LIFE HAVE YOU MISSED? SHOES? AUTOMOBILES? TWO-PLY TOILET PAPER? WE DIGRESS.

THIS VACATION BIN·GO GAME IS PLAYED MUCH LIKE THE TRADITIONAL ONE. YOUR GOAL IS TO SIMPLY BE THE FIRST TO FILL 5 SEQUENTIAL SQUARES IN A ROW, A COLUMN, OR EVEN DIAGONALLY (SEE FIGURE 1 BELOW).

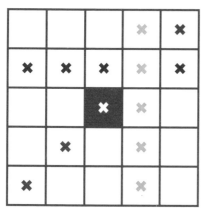

FIGURE 1

SEE THAT X IN THE CENTER SQUARE OF YOUR BOARDS? THAT'S A FREE SQUARE—WHICH MEANS EVERY PLAYER GETS THIS ONE AUTOMATICALLY. IT REALLY HELPS SO...YOU'RE WELCOME.

PLAYING THE GAME

AFTER DETERMINING HOW MANY PEOPLE ARE PLAYING, THE OWNER OF THE BOOK SHOULD PERF. OUT A CARD (OR TWO) FOR EVERYONE TO USE AS THEIR PLAY BOARD(S).

ALRIGHT, SO HERE'S HOW OUR GAME IS A BIT DIFFERENT. WE'VE PRE-FILLED EACH CARD WITH THE COMMON (YET RIDICULOUS) THINGS THAT ALWAYS SEEM TO HAPPEN WHILE TRAVELING. SO, INSTEAD OF SOMEONE JUST CALLING OUT NUMBERS, EVERYONE IS PEOPLE WATCHING INSTEAD. WHEN SOMETHING HAPPENS THAT IS ON ONE OF YOUR SQUARES, YOU CALL IT OUT (AS DISCREETLY AS APPROPRIATE, OF COURSE) AND MARK OFF THE SQUARE.

JUST REMEMBER THAT THE OTHER PLAYERS NEED TO BE AWARE OF THE 'CALL'—AND IDEALLY SEE IT AS WELL (BUT THAT'S NOT A REQUIREMENT). THAT WAY THEY CAN ALSO MARK OFF THAT SQUARE IF IT'S ON THEIR BOARD.

WINNING

WHEN A PLAYER MARKS OFF A WINNING CARD, THEY SHOULD ANNOUNCE 'BINGO.' IN THE EVENT OF A TIE, THE FIRST TO SAY IT IS THE WINNER. EITHER WAY—EVERYONE ELSE IN THE ROOM WILL PROBABLY BE WONDERING WHAT THE HELL YOU ARE DOING. ADMITTEDLY IT MIGHT BE HARD TO MAKE A TRUE BINGO, SO YOU CAN ALSO DECIDE THAT THE PLAYER WITH THE MOST SQUARES MARKED OFF IS THE WINNER.

BONUS: YOU CAN ALSO PLAY THIS AS A DRINKING GAME. IT'S SIMPLE. WHEN SOMETHING HAPPENS ON YOUR CARD, YOU HAVE TO TAKE A DRINK (AFTER TRAVELING IS DONE OF COURSE). IF YOU MAKE A BINGO—WELL NOW EVERYONE ELSE HAS TO DRINK. JUST TALLY UP DRINKS ONCE YOU'RE AT YOUR DESTINATION & GO TO THE BAR.

ROAD TRIP BIN×GO ROAD TRIP

THERE'S A NON-PIZZA BUSINESS OPERATING IN AN OLD PIZZA HUT.	A ROADSIDE 'ATTRACTION' LOOKS LIKE IT'S BEEN CLOSED FOR 100 YEARS.	A LANE IS CLOSED FOR REPAIRS—THAT NO ONE IS ACTUALLY WORKING ON.	A MINIVAN HAS THEMED STICKERS REPRESENTING AN ENORMOUS FAMILY.	A VEHICLE PLASTERED IN NONSENSICAL BUMPER STICKERS IS SPOTTED.
A ROADSIDE BILLBOARD ADVERTISES THE WORLD'S BEST FUDGE.	A MOTEL ADVERTISES THAT IT HAS COLOR TELEVISION.	THERE'S A WESTERN WEAR STORE—NOT EVEN CLOSE TO THE ACTUAL WEST.	AN ACTUAL TUMBLEWEED BLOWS ACROSS THE ROAD.	A TRUCK STOP HAS ITS OWN EATING CHALLENGE FOR A FREE T-SHIRT.
THERE'S A QUIRKY BILLBOARD FOR A PREDATORY LAWYER.	A ROADSIDE FRUIT STAND IS SELLING QUESTIONABLE PRODUCE.	✖	ANOTHER CAR'S BLINKER IS LEFT ON FOR MILES.	AN OLD SCHOOL BUS HAS BEEN CONVERTED INTO AN RV.
SOMEONE IS HAULING A BROKEN DOWN COUCH THAT ISN'T EVEN TIED DOWN.	EVERYONE SUDDENLY STARTS GOING THE SPEED LIMIT BECAUSE OF A COP.	THERE'S A MOTORCYCLE THAT'S THE SIZE OF A SMALL CAR.	A TOWN CONSISTS OF A DINER AND A GAS STATION—THAT BOTH CLOSE AT 6.	A HOMEMADE BILLBOARD SPICES UP THE LANDSCAPE OF A LOCAL CORNFIELD.
A CAR IS SO PACKED FULL OF JUNK THAT ALL OF THE WINDOWS ARE BLOCKED.	SOMEONE IS 'DRIVING' A HORSE AND BUGGY ON THE HIGHWAY.	THE PHRASE 'ARE WE THERE YET?' IS UTTERED.	AN 'ADULT SUPERSTORE' IS LOCATED RIGHT BESIDE A FIREWORKS SHOP.	A CAR USING A TINY SPARE TIRE PASSES YOU AT 85 MPH.

BIN×GO

OBJECTIVE

OH, YOU MEAN BESIDES TRYING TO PASS THE TIME DURING THIS VACATION THAT YOU MAY OR MAY NOT HAVE EVEN WANTED TO GO ON? ISN'T THAT ENOUGH? WHAT DO YOU WANT FROM US?

WELL, WE HOPE YOU'RE AT LEAST FAMILIAR WITH THE CONCEPT OF BINGO. BECAUSE IF NOT, WELL WE ARE REALLY KIND OF WORRIED ABOUT YOU. WHAT OTHER THINGS IN LIFE HAVE YOU MISSED? SHOES? AUTOMOBILES? TWO-PLY TOILET PAPER? WE DIGRESS.

THIS VACATION BIN·GO GAME IS PLAYED MUCH LIKE THE TRADITIONAL ONE. YOUR GOAL IS TO SIMPLY BE THE FIRST TO FILL 5 SEQUENTIAL SQUARES IN A ROW, A COLUMN, OR EVEN DIAGONALLY (SEE FIGURE 1 BELOW).

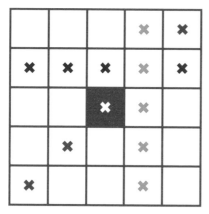

FIGURE 1

SEE THAT X IN THE CENTER SQUARE OF YOUR BOARDS? THAT'S A FREE SQUARE—WHICH MEANS EVERY PLAYER GETS THIS ONE AUTOMATICALLY. IT REALLY HELPS SO...YOU'RE WELCOME.

PLAYING THE GAME

AFTER DETERMINING HOW MANY PEOPLE ARE PLAYING, THE OWNER OF THE BOOK SHOULD PERF. OUT A CARD (OR TWO) FOR EVERYONE TO USE AS THEIR PLAY BOARD(S).

ALRIGHT, SO HERE'S HOW OUR GAME IS A BIT DIFFERENT. WE'VE PRE-FILLED EACH CARD WITH THE COMMON (YET RIDICULOUS) THINGS THAT ALWAYS SEEM TO HAPPEN WHILE TRAVELING. SO, INSTEAD OF SOMEONE JUST CALLING OUT NUMBERS, EVERYONE IS PEOPLE WATCHING INSTEAD. WHEN SOMETHING HAPPENS THAT IS ON ONE OF YOUR SQUARES, YOU CALL IT OUT (AS DISCREETLY AS APPROPRIATE, OF COURSE) AND MARK OFF THE SQUARE.

JUST REMEMBER THAT THE OTHER PLAYERS NEED TO BE AWARE OF THE 'CALL'—AND IDEALLY SEE IT AS WELL (BUT THAT'S NOT A REQUIREMENT). THAT WAY THEY CAN ALSO MARK OFF THAT SQUARE IF IT'S ON THEIR BOARD.

WINNING

WHEN A PLAYER MARKS OFF A WINNING CARD, THEY SHOULD ANNOUNCE 'BINGO.' IN THE EVENT OF A TIE, THE FIRST TO SAY IT IS THE WINNER. EITHER WAY—EVERYONE ELSE IN THE ROOM WILL PROBABLY BE WONDERING WHAT THE HELL YOU ARE DOING. ADMITTEDLY IT MIGHT BE HARD TO MAKE A TRUE BINGO, SO YOU CAN ALSO DECIDE THAT THE PLAYER WITH THE MOST SQUARES MARKED OFF IS THE WINNER.

BONUS: YOU CAN ALSO PLAY THIS AS A DRINKING GAME. IT'S SIMPLE. WHEN SOMETHING HAPPENS ON YOUR CARD, YOU HAVE TO TAKE A DRINK (AFTER TRAVELING IS DONE OF COURSE). IF YOU MAKE A BINGO—WELL NOW EVERYONE ELSE HAS TO DRINK. JUST TALLY UP DRINKS ONCE YOU'RE AT YOUR DESTINATION & GO TO THE BAR.

THERE'S A NON-PIZZA BUSINESS OPERATING IN AN OLD PIZZA HUT.	THERE'S A QUIRKY BILLBOARD FOR A PREDATORY LAWYER.	GAS STATION HOT DOGS APPEAR TO HAVE BEEN ON THE ROLLERS SINCE 2012.	THERE'S A CAR WITH A SET OF EYELASHES ON THE HEADLIGHTS.	THE PHRASE 'ARE WE THERE YET?' IS UTTERED.
AN OPEN-BED TRUCK HAS A DOG AND/OR CHILD RIDING IN THE BACK.	A LANE IS CLOSED FOR REPAIRS—THAT NO ONE IS ACTUALLY WORKING ON.	A STATE REST STOP IS USED WITHOUT EVEN BEING MURDERED.	SOMEONE IS GOING 20 MILES UNDER THE SPEED LIMIT IN THE FAST LANE.	MALE GENITALIA IS FEATURED AS 'DECOR' ON THE BACK OF A TRUCK.
A CAR HAS WILDLY EXPIRED TEMPORARY TAGS.	SOMEONE IS 'DRIVING' A HORSE AND BUGGY ON THE HIGHWAY.	✖	A MINIVAN HAS THEMED STICKERS REPRESENTING AN ENORMOUS FAMILY.	SOMEONE IS WALKING ON THE SIDE OF THE HIGHWAY.
A ROADSIDE FRUIT STAND IS SELLING QUESTIONABLE PRODUCE.	A SLOW CAR STARTS TO SPEED UP THE MOMENT THAT SOMEONE TRIES TO PASS.	AN 80 YEAR-OLD MAN IS DRIVING AN RV BIGGER THAN MOST HOUSES.	BATHROOMS AT THE GAS STATION ARE TOO GROSS TO USE.	A CAR USING A TINY SPARE TIRE PASSES YOU AT 85 MPH.
A DIGITAL ROAD SIGN DISPLAYS A 'JOKE' ABOUT TRAFFIC SAFETY.	AN ACTUAL HITCHHIKER IS SEEN—DESPITE IT NOT BEING 1974.	A ROADSIDE BILLBOARD ADVERTISES THE WORLD'S BEST FUDGE.	A TOWN CONSISTS OF A DINER AND A GAS STATION— THAT BOTH CLOSE AT 6.	A CONFUSING PERSONALIZED LICENSE PLATE IS SPOTTED.

OBJECTIVE

OH, YOU MEAN BESIDES TRYING TO PASS THE TIME DURING THIS VACATION THAT YOU MAY OR MAY NOT HAVE EVEN WANTED TO GO ON? ISN'T THAT ENOUGH? WHAT DO YOU WANT FROM US?

WELL, WE HOPE YOU'RE AT LEAST FAMILIAR WITH THE CONCEPT OF BINGO. BECAUSE IF NOT, WELL WE ARE REALLY KIND OF WORRIED ABOUT YOU. WHAT OTHER THINGS IN LIFE HAVE YOU MISSED? SHOES? AUTOMOBILES? TWO-PLY TOILET PAPER? WE DIGRESS.

THIS VACATION BIN·GO GAME IS PLAYED MUCH LIKE THE TRADITIONAL ONE. YOUR GOAL IS TO SIMPLY BE THE FIRST TO FILL 5 SEQUENTIAL SQUARES IN A ROW, A COLUMN, OR EVEN DIAGONALLY (SEE FIGURE 1 BELOW).

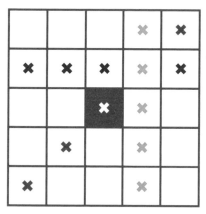

FIGURE 1

SEE THAT X IN THE CENTER SQUARE OF YOUR BOARDS? THAT'S A FREE SQUARE—WHICH MEANS EVERY PLAYER GETS THIS ONE AUTOMATICALLY. IT REALLY HELPS SO...YOU'RE WELCOME.

PLAYING THE GAME

AFTER DETERMINING HOW MANY PEOPLE ARE PLAYING, THE OWNER OF THE BOOK SHOULD PERF. OUT A CARD (OR TWO) FOR EVERYONE TO USE AS THEIR PLAY BOARD(S).

ALRIGHT, SO HERE'S HOW OUR GAME IS A BIT DIFFERENT. WE'VE PRE-FILLED EACH CARD WITH THE COMMON (YET RIDICULOUS) THINGS THAT ALWAYS SEEM TO HAPPEN WHILE TRAVELING. SO, INSTEAD OF SOMEONE JUST CALLING OUT NUMBERS, EVERYONE IS PEOPLE WATCHING INSTEAD. WHEN SOMETHING HAPPENS THAT IS ON ONE OF YOUR SQUARES, YOU CALL IT OUT (AS DISCREETLY AS APPROPRIATE, OF COURSE) AND MARK OFF THE SQUARE.

JUST REMEMBER THAT THE OTHER PLAYERS NEED TO BE AWARE OF THE 'CALL'—AND IDEALLY SEE IT AS WELL (BUT THAT'S NOT A REQUIREMENT). THAT WAY THEY CAN ALSO MARK OFF THAT SQUARE IF IT'S ON THEIR BOARD.

WINNING

WHEN A PLAYER MARKS OFF A WINNING CARD, THEY SHOULD ANNOUNCE 'BINGO.' IN THE EVENT OF A TIE, THE FIRST TO SAY IT IS THE WINNER. EITHER WAY—EVERYONE ELSE IN THE ROOM WILL PROBABLY BE WONDERING WHAT THE HELL YOU ARE DOING. ADMITTEDLY IT MIGHT BE HARD TO MAKE A TRUE BINGO, SO YOU CAN ALSO DECIDE THAT THE PLAYER WITH THE MOST SQUARES MARKED OFF IS THE WINNER.

BONUS: YOU CAN ALSO PLAY THIS AS A DRINKING GAME. IT'S SIMPLE. WHEN SOMETHING HAPPENS ON YOUR CARD, YOU HAVE TO TAKE A DRINK (AFTER TRAVELING IS DONE OF COURSE). IF YOU MAKE A BINGO—WELL NOW EVERYONE ELSE HAS TO DRINK. JUST TALLY UP DRINKS ONCE YOU'RE AT YOUR DESTINATION & GO TO THE BAR.

ROAD TRIP BIN×GO ROAD TRIP

A CAR HAS WILDLY EXPIRED TEMPORARY TAGS.	A TOWN WATER TOWER IS PAINTED TO LOOK LIKE SOMETHING KITSCHY.	GAS STATION HOT DOGS APPEAR TO HAVE BEEN ON THE ROLLERS SINCE 2012.	A DIGITAL ROAD SIGN DISPLAYS A 'JOKE' ABOUT TRAFFIC SAFETY.	A VEHICLE PLASTERED IN NONSENSICAL BUMPER STICKERS IS SPOTTED.
AN OLD SCHOOL BUS HAS BEEN CONVERTED INTO AN RV.	A CAR IS SO PACKED FULL OF JUNK THAT ALL OF THE WINDOWS ARE BLOCKED.	'ON THE ROAD AGAIN' IS SAID/SUNG AFTER A PIT STOP.	A CAR USING A TINY SPARE TIRE PASSES YOU AT 85 MPH.	SOMEONE AT THE GAS STATION IS LITERALLY WEARING PAJAMAS.
THERE'S A CASINO INSIDE OF A GAS STATION.	A STATE REST STOP IS USED WITHOUT EVEN BEING MURDERED.	✖	SOMEONE IS GOING 20 MILES UNDER THE SPEED LIMIT IN THE FAST LANE.	A SLOW CAR STARTS TO SPEED UP THE MOMENT THAT SOMEONE TRIES TO PASS.
AN ACTUAL TUMBLEWEED BLOWS ACROSS THE ROAD.	SOMEONE IS 'DRIVING' A HORSE AND BUGGY ON THE HIGHWAY.	THERE'S AN OVER-SIZED LOAD HAULING MYSTERY EQUIPMENT AT 35 MPH.	'CLEAN ME' IS WRITTEN IN DIRT ON A PASSING VEHICLE.	AN 80 YEAR-OLD MAN IS DRIVING AN RV BIGGER THAN MOST HOUSES.
THERE'S A CAR WITH A SET OF EYELASHES ON THE HEADLIGHTS.	A MINIVAN HAS THEMED STICKERS REPRESENTING AN ENORMOUS FAMILY.	A LIVESTOCK TRAILER IS SMELLED BEFORE IT IS SEEN.	BATHROOMS AT THE GAS STATION ARE TOO GROSS TO USE.	THERE'S A MOTORCYCLE THAT'S THE SIZE OF A SMALL CAR.

OBJECTIVE

OH, YOU MEAN BESIDES TRYING TO PASS THE TIME DURING THIS VACATION THAT YOU MAY OR MAY NOT HAVE EVEN WANTED TO GO ON? ISN'T THAT ENOUGH? WHAT DO YOU WANT FROM US?

WELL, WE HOPE YOU'RE AT LEAST FAMILIAR WITH THE CONCEPT OF BINGO. BECAUSE IF NOT, WELL WE ARE REALLY KIND OF WORRIED ABOUT YOU. WHAT OTHER THINGS IN LIFE HAVE YOU MISSED? SHOES? AUTOMOBILES? TWO-PLY TOILET PAPER? WE DIGRESS.

THIS VACATION BIN·GO GAME IS PLAYED MUCH LIKE THE TRADITIONAL ONE. YOUR GOAL IS TO SIMPLY BE THE FIRST TO FILL 5 SEQUENTIAL SQUARES IN A ROW, A COLUMN, OR EVEN DIAGONALLY (SEE FIGURE 1 BELOW).

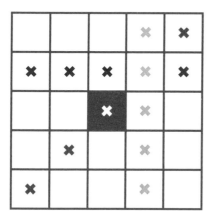

FIGURE 1

SEE THAT X IN THE CENTER SQUARE OF YOUR BOARDS? THAT'S A FREE SQUARE–WHICH MEANS EVERY PLAYER GETS THIS ONE AUTOMATICALLY. IT REALLY HELPS SO...YOU'RE WELCOME.

PLAYING THE GAME

AFTER DETERMINING HOW MANY PEOPLE ARE PLAYING, THE OWNER OF THE BOOK SHOULD PERF. OUT A CARD (OR TWO) FOR EVERYONE TO USE AS THEIR PLAY BOARD(S).

ALRIGHT, SO HERE'S HOW OUR GAME IS A BIT DIFFERENT. WE'VE PRE-FILLED EACH CARD WITH THE COMMON (YET RIDICULOUS) THINGS THAT ALWAYS SEEM TO HAPPEN WHILE TRAVELING. SO, INSTEAD OF SOMEONE JUST CALLING OUT NUMBERS, EVERYONE IS PEOPLE WATCHING INSTEAD. WHEN SOMETHING HAPPENS THAT IS ON ONE OF YOUR SQUARES, YOU CALL IT OUT (AS DISCREETLY AS APPROPRIATE, OF COURSE) AND MARK OFF THE SQUARE.

JUST REMEMBER THAT THE OTHER PLAYERS NEED TO BE AWARE OF THE 'CALL'–AND IDEALLY SEE IT AS WELL (BUT THAT'S NOT A REQUIREMENT). THAT WAY THEY CAN ALSO MARK OFF THAT SQUARE IF IT'S ON THEIR BOARD.

WINNING

WHEN A PLAYER MARKS OFF A WINNING CARD, THEY SHOULD ANNOUNCE 'BINGO.' IN THE EVENT OF A TIE, THE FIRST TO SAY IT IS THE WINNER. EITHER WAY–EVERYONE ELSE IN THE ROOM WILL PROBABLY BE WONDERING WHAT THE HELL YOU ARE DOING. ADMITTEDLY IT MIGHT BE HARD TO MAKE A TRUE BINGO, SO YOU CAN ALSO DECIDE THAT THE PLAYER WITH THE MOST SQUARES MARKED OFF IS THE WINNER.

BONUS: YOU CAN ALSO PLAY THIS AS A DRINKING GAME. IT'S SIMPLE. WHEN SOMETHING HAPPENS ON YOUR CARD, YOU HAVE TO TAKE A DRINK (AFTER TRAVELING IS DONE OF COURSE). IF YOU MAKE A BINGO–WELL NOW EVERYONE ELSE HAS TO DRINK. JUST TALLY UP DRINKS ONCE YOU'RE AT YOUR DESTINATION & GO TO THE BAR.

A TOWN CONSISTS OF A DINER AND A GAS STATION—THAT BOTH CLOSE AT 6.	SOMEONE AT THE GAS STATION IS LITERALLY WEARING PAJAMAS.	SOMEONE IS HAULING A BROKEN DOWN COUCH THAT ISN'T EVEN TIED DOWN.	A MOTEL ADVERTISES THAT IT HAS COLOR TELEVISION.	A CAR USING A TINY SPARE TIRE PASSES YOU AT 85 MPH.
A VEHICLE PLASTERED IN NONSENSICAL BUMPER STICKERS IS SPOTTED.	A LIVESTOCK TRAILER IS SMELLED BEFORE IT IS SEEN.	EVERYONE SUDDENLY STARTS GOING THE SPEED LIMIT BECAUSE OF A COP.	SOMEONE IS GOING 20 MILES UNDER THE SPEED LIMIT IN THE FAST LANE.	A CAR HAS WILDLY EXPIRED TEMPORARY TAGS.
A ROADSIDE BILLBOARD ADVERTISES THE WORLD'S BEST FUDGE.	A SLOW CAR STARTS TO SPEED UP THE MOMENT THAT SOMEONE TRIES TO PASS.	✖	THERE'S A MOTORCYCLE THAT'S THE SIZE OF A SMALL CAR.	SOMEONE IS 'DRIVING' A HORSE AND BUGGY ON THE HIGHWAY.
'ON THE ROAD AGAIN' IS SAID/SUNG AFTER A PIT STOP.	A LANE IS CLOSED FOR REPAIRS—THAT NO ONE IS ACTUALLY WORKING ON.	THE RADIO STATION JUST TURNS INTO STATIC.	THERE'S A CASINO INSIDE OF A GAS STATION.	A ROADSIDE 'ATTRACTION' LOOKS LIKE IT'S BEEN CLOSED FOR 100 YEARS.
AN ACTUAL HITCHHIKER IS SEEN—DESPITE IT NOT BEING 1974.	A STATE REST STOP IS USED WITHOUT EVEN BEING MURDERED.	A ROADSIDE FRUIT STAND IS SELLING QUESTIONABLE PRODUCE.	A BUNCH OF OLD-TIMEY CARS APPEAR OUT OF NOWHERE ON THE HIGHWAY.	A HOMEMADE BILLBOARD SPICES UP THE LANDSCAPE OF A LOCAL CORNFIELD.

OBJECTIVE

OH, YOU MEAN BESIDES TRYING TO PASS THE TIME DURING THIS VACATION THAT YOU MAY OR MAY NOT HAVE EVEN WANTED TO GO ON? ISN'T THAT ENOUGH? WHAT DO YOU WANT FROM US?

WELL, WE HOPE YOU'RE AT LEAST FAMILIAR WITH THE CONCEPT OF BINGO. BECAUSE IF NOT, WELL WE ARE REALLY KIND OF WORRIED ABOUT YOU. WHAT OTHER THINGS IN LIFE HAVE YOU MISSED? SHOES? AUTOMOBILES? TWO-PLY TOILET PAPER? WE DIGRESS.

THIS VACATION BIN·GO GAME IS PLAYED MUCH LIKE THE TRADITIONAL ONE. YOUR GOAL IS TO SIMPLY BE THE FIRST TO FILL 5 SEQUENTIAL SQUARES IN A ROW, A COLUMN, OR EVEN DIAGONALLY (SEE FIGURE 1 BELOW).

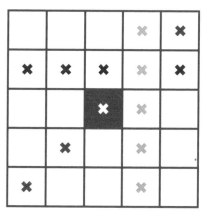

FIGURE 1

SEE THAT X IN THE CENTER SQUARE OF YOUR BOARDS? THAT'S A FREE SQUARE—WHICH MEANS EVERY PLAYER GETS THIS ONE AUTOMATICALLY. IT REALLY HELPS SO...YOU'RE WELCOME.

PLAYING THE GAME

AFTER DETERMINING HOW MANY PEOPLE ARE PLAYING, THE OWNER OF THE BOOK SHOULD PERF. OUT A CARD (OR TWO) FOR EVERYONE TO USE AS THEIR PLAY BOARD(S).

ALRIGHT, SO HERE'S HOW OUR GAME IS A BIT DIFFERENT. WE'VE PRE-FILLED EACH CARD WITH THE COMMON (YET RIDICULOUS) THINGS THAT ALWAYS SEEM TO HAPPEN WHILE TRAVELING. SO, INSTEAD OF SOMEONE JUST CALLING OUT NUMBERS, EVERYONE IS PEOPLE WATCHING INSTEAD. WHEN SOMETHING HAPPENS THAT IS ON ONE OF YOUR SQUARES, YOU CALL IT OUT (AS DISCREETLY AS APPROPRIATE, OF COURSE) AND MARK OFF THE SQUARE.

JUST REMEMBER THAT THE OTHER PLAYERS NEED TO BE AWARE OF THE 'CALL'—AND IDEALLY SEE IT AS WELL (BUT THAT'S NOT A REQUIREMENT). THAT WAY THEY CAN ALSO MARK OFF THAT SQUARE IF IT'S ON THEIR BOARD.

WINNING

WHEN A PLAYER MARKS OFF A WINNING CARD, THEY SHOULD ANNOUNCE 'BINGO.' IN THE EVENT OF A TIE, THE FIRST TO SAY IT IS THE WINNER. EITHER WAY—EVERYONE ELSE IN THE ROOM WILL PROBABLY BE WONDERING WHAT THE HELL YOU ARE DOING. ADMITTEDLY IT MIGHT BE HARD TO MAKE A TRUE BINGO, SO YOU CAN ALSO DECIDE THAT THE PLAYER WITH THE MOST SQUARES MARKED OFF IS THE WINNER.

BONUS: YOU CAN ALSO PLAY THIS AS A DRINKING GAME. IT'S SIMPLE. WHEN SOMETHING HAPPENS ON YOUR CARD, YOU HAVE TO TAKE A DRINK (AFTER TRAVELING IS DONE OF COURSE). IF YOU MAKE A BINGO—WELL NOW EVERYONE ELSE HAS TO DRINK. JUST TALLY UP DRINKS ONCE YOU'RE AT YOUR DESTINATION & GO TO THE BAR.

EVERYONE SUDDENLY STARTS GOING THE SPEED LIMIT BECAUSE OF A COP.	A CAR IS SO PACKED FULL OF JUNK THAT ALL OF THE WINDOWS ARE BLOCKED.	A TOWN CONSISTS OF A DINER AND A GAS STATION—THAT BOTH CLOSE AT 6.	A CONFUSING PERSONALIZED LICENSE PLATE IS SPOTTED.	SOMEONE IS WALKING ON THE SIDE OF THE HIGHWAY.
A PASSENGER HAS THEIR BARE FEET ON THE DASHBOARD OF A CAR.	AN OPEN-BED TRUCK HAS A DOG AND/OR CHILD RIDING IN THE BACK.	'ON THE ROAD AGAIN' IS SAID/SUNG AFTER A PIT STOP.	THERE'S A MOTORCYCLE THAT'S THE SIZE OF A SMALL CAR.	A ROADSIDE 'ATTRACTION' LOOKS LIKE IT'S BEEN CLOSED FOR 100 YEARS.
MALE GENITALIA IS FEATURED AS 'DECOR' ON THE BACK OF A TRUCK.	THERE'S A CAR WITH A SET OF EYELASHES ON THE HEADLIGHTS.	✖	'CLEAN ME' IS WRITTEN IN DIRT ON A PASSING VEHICLE.	A LANE IS CLOSED FOR REPAIRS—THAT NO ONE IS ACTUALLY WORKING ON.
A ROADSIDE FRUIT STAND IS SELLING QUESTIONABLE PRODUCE.	THERE'S A NON-PIZZA BUSINESS OPERATING IN AN OLD PIZZA HUT.	BATHROOMS AT THE GAS STATION ARE TOO GROSS TO USE.	A TRUCK STOP HAS ITS OWN EATING CHALLENGE FOR A FREE T-SHIRT.	SOMEONE AT THE GAS STATION IS LITERALLY WEARING PAJAMAS.
AN OLD SCHOOL BUS HAS BEEN CONVERTED INTO AN RV.	ANOTHER CAR'S BLINKER IS LEFT ON FOR MILES.	GAS STATION HOT DOGS APPEAR TO HAVE BEEN ON THE ROLLERS SINCE 2012.	THERE'S A QUIRKY BILLBOARD FOR A PREDATORY LAWYER.	AN 'ADULT SUPERSTORE' IS LOCATED RIGHT BESIDE A FIREWORKS SHOP.

OBJECTIVE

OH, YOU MEAN BESIDES TRYING TO PASS THE TIME DURING THIS VACATION THAT YOU MAY OR MAY NOT HAVE EVEN WANTED TO GO ON? ISN'T THAT ENOUGH? WHAT DO YOU WANT FROM US?

WELL, WE HOPE YOU'RE AT LEAST FAMILIAR WITH THE CONCEPT OF BINGO. BECAUSE IF NOT, WELL WE ARE REALLY KIND OF WORRIED ABOUT YOU. WHAT OTHER THINGS IN LIFE HAVE YOU MISSED? SHOES? AUTOMOBILES? TWO-PLY TOILET PAPER? WE DIGRESS.

THIS VACATION BIN·GO GAME IS PLAYED MUCH LIKE THE TRADITIONAL ONE. YOUR GOAL IS TO SIMPLY BE THE FIRST TO FILL 5 SEQUENTIAL SQUARES IN A ROW, A COLUMN, OR EVEN DIAGONALLY (SEE FIGURE 1 BELOW).

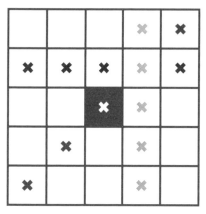

FIGURE 1

SEE THAT X IN THE CENTER SQUARE OF YOUR BOARDS? THAT'S A FREE SQUARE—WHICH MEANS EVERY PLAYER GETS THIS ONE AUTOMATICALLY. IT REALLY HELPS SO...YOU'RE WELCOME.

PLAYING THE GAME

AFTER DETERMINING HOW MANY PEOPLE ARE PLAYING, THE OWNER OF THE BOOK SHOULD PERF. OUT A CARD (OR TWO) FOR EVERYONE TO USE AS THEIR PLAY BOARD(S).

ALRIGHT, SO HERE'S HOW OUR GAME IS A BIT DIFFERENT. WE'VE PRE-FILLED EACH CARD WITH THE COMMON (YET RIDICULOUS) THINGS THAT ALWAYS SEEM TO HAPPEN WHILE TRAVELING. SO, INSTEAD OF SOMEONE JUST CALLING OUT NUMBERS, EVERYONE IS PEOPLE WATCHING INSTEAD. WHEN SOMETHING HAPPENS THAT IS ON ONE OF YOUR SQUARES, YOU CALL IT OUT (AS DISCREETLY AS APPROPRIATE, OF COURSE) AND MARK OFF THE SQUARE.

JUST REMEMBER THAT THE OTHER PLAYERS NEED TO BE AWARE OF THE 'CALL'—AND IDEALLY SEE IT AS WELL (BUT THAT'S NOT A REQUIREMENT). THAT WAY THEY CAN ALSO MARK OFF THAT SQUARE IF IT'S ON THEIR BOARD.

WINNING

WHEN A PLAYER MARKS OFF A WINNING CARD, THEY SHOULD ANNOUNCE 'BINGO.' IN THE EVENT OF A TIE, THE FIRST TO SAY IT IS THE WINNER. EITHER WAY—EVERYONE ELSE IN THE ROOM WILL PROBABLY BE WONDERING WHAT THE HELL YOU ARE DOING. ADMITTEDLY IT MIGHT BE HARD TO MAKE A TRUE BINGO, SO YOU CAN ALSO DECIDE THAT THE PLAYER WITH THE MOST SQUARES MARKED OFF IS THE WINNER.

BONUS: YOU CAN ALSO PLAY THIS AS A DRINKING GAME. IT'S SIMPLE. WHEN SOMETHING HAPPENS ON YOUR CARD, YOU HAVE TO TAKE A DRINK (AFTER TRAVELING IS DONE OF COURSE). IF YOU MAKE A BINGO—WELL NOW EVERYONE ELSE HAS TO DRINK. JUST TALLY UP DRINKS ONCE YOU'RE AT YOUR DESTINATION & GO TO THE BAR.

A TOWN WATER TOWER IS PAINTED TO LOOK LIKE SOMETHING KITSCHY.	AN OLD SCHOOL BUS HAS BEEN CONVERTED INTO AN RV.	A PASSENGER HAS THEIR BARE FEET ON THE DASHBOARD OF A CAR.	THE PHRASE 'ARE WE THERE YET?' IS UTTERED.	ANOTHER CAR'S BLINKER IS LEFT ON FOR MILES.
AN ACTUAL TUMBLEWEED BLOWS ACROSS THE ROAD.	A CAR HAS WILDLY EXPIRED TEMPORARY TAGS.	'ON THE ROAD AGAIN' IS SAID/SUNG AFTER A PIT STOP.	A BUNCH OF OLD-TIMEY CARS APPEAR OUT OF NOWHERE ON THE HIGHWAY.	A TRUCK STOP HAS ITS OWN EATING CHALLENGE FOR A FREE T-SHIRT.
A ROADSIDE FRUIT STAND IS SELLING QUESTIONABLE PRODUCE.	A MOTEL ADVERTISES THAT IT HAS COLOR TELEVISION.	✖	A MINIVAN HAS THEMED STICKERS REPRESENTING AN ENORMOUS FAMILY.	AN ACTUAL HITCHHIKER IS SEEN—DESPITE IT NOT BEING 1974.
GAS STATION HOT DOGS APPEAR TO HAVE BEEN ON THE ROLLERS SINCE 2012.	THERE'S A QUIRKY BILLBOARD FOR A PREDATORY LAWYER.	THERE'S A CASINO INSIDE OF A GAS STATION.	THERE'S AN OVER-SIZED LOAD HAULING MYSTERY EQUIPMENT AT 35 MPH.	A HOMEMADE BILLBOARD SPICES UP THE LANDSCAPE OF A LOCAL CORNFIELD.
A CAR IS SO PACKED FULL OF JUNK THAT ALL OF THE WINDOWS ARE BLOCKED.	THERE'S A MOTORCYCLE THAT'S THE SIZE OF A SMALL CAR.	A STATE REST STOP IS USED WITHOUT EVEN BEING MURDERED.	'CLEAN ME' IS WRITTEN IN DIRT ON A PASSING VEHICLE.	A ROADSIDE BILLBOARD ADVERTISES THE WORLD'S BEST FUDGE.

OBJECTIVE

OH, YOU MEAN BESIDES TRYING TO PASS THE TIME DURING THIS VACATION THAT YOU MAY OR MAY NOT HAVE EVEN WANTED TO GO ON? ISN'T THAT ENOUGH? WHAT DO YOU WANT FROM US?

WELL, WE HOPE YOU'RE AT LEAST FAMILIAR WITH THE CONCEPT OF BINGO. BECAUSE IF NOT, WELL WE ARE REALLY KIND OF WORRIED ABOUT YOU. WHAT OTHER THINGS IN LIFE HAVE YOU MISSED? SHOES? AUTOMOBILES? TWO-PLY TOILET PAPER? WE DIGRESS.

THIS VACATION BIN×GO GAME IS PLAYED MUCH LIKE THE TRADITIONAL ONE. YOUR GOAL IS TO SIMPLY BE THE FIRST TO FILL 5 SEQUENTIAL SQUARES IN A ROW, A COLUMN, OR EVEN DIAGONALLY (SEE FIGURE 1 BELOW).

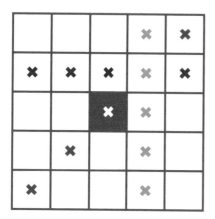

FIGURE 1

SEE THAT X IN THE CENTER SQUARE OF YOUR BOARDS? THAT'S A FREE SQUARE—WHICH MEANS EVERY PLAYER GETS THIS ONE AUTOMATICALLY. IT REALLY HELPS SO...YOU'RE WELCOME.

PLAYING THE GAME

AFTER DETERMINING HOW MANY PEOPLE ARE PLAYING, THE OWNER OF THE BOOK SHOULD PERF. OUT A CARD (OR TWO) FOR EVERYONE TO USE AS THEIR PLAY BOARD(S).

ALRIGHT, SO HERE'S HOW OUR GAME IS A BIT DIFFERENT. WE'VE PRE-FILLED EACH CARD WITH THE COMMON (YET RIDICULOUS) THINGS THAT ALWAYS SEEM TO HAPPEN WHILE TRAVELING. SO, INSTEAD OF SOMEONE JUST CALLING OUT NUMBERS, EVERYONE IS PEOPLE WATCHING INSTEAD. WHEN SOMETHING HAPPENS THAT IS ON ONE OF YOUR SQUARES, YOU CALL IT OUT (AS DISCREETLY AS APPROPRIATE, OF COURSE) AND MARK OFF THE SQUARE.

JUST REMEMBER THAT THE OTHER PLAYERS NEED TO BE AWARE OF THE 'CALL'—AND IDEALLY SEE IT AS WELL (BUT THAT'S NOT A REQUIREMENT). THAT WAY THEY CAN ALSO MARK OFF THAT SQUARE IF IT'S ON THEIR BOARD.

WINNING

WHEN A PLAYER MARKS OFF A WINNING CARD, THEY SHOULD ANNOUNCE 'BINGO.' IN THE EVENT OF A TIE, THE FIRST TO SAY IT IS THE WINNER. EITHER WAY—EVERYONE ELSE IN THE ROOM WILL PROBABLY BE WONDERING WHAT THE HELL YOU ARE DOING. ADMITTEDLY IT MIGHT BE HARD TO MAKE A TRUE BINGO, SO YOU CAN ALSO DECIDE THAT THE PLAYER WITH THE MOST SQUARES MARKED OFF IS THE WINNER.

BONUS: YOU CAN ALSO PLAY THIS AS A DRINKING GAME. IT'S SIMPLE. WHEN SOMETHING HAPPENS ON YOUR CARD, YOU HAVE TO TAKE A DRINK (AFTER TRAVELING IS DONE OF COURSE). IF YOU MAKE A BINGO—WELL NOW EVERYONE ELSE HAS TO DRINK. JUST TALLY UP DRINKS ONCE YOU'RE AT YOUR DESTINATION & GO TO THE BAR.

THERE'S A NON-PIZZA BUSINESS OPERATING IN AN OLD PIZZA HUT.	THE PHRASE 'ARE WE THERE YET?' IS UTTERED.	A MOTEL ADVERTISES THAT IT HAS COLOR TELEVISION.	SOMEONE IS HAULING A BROKEN DOWN COUCH THAT ISN'T EVEN TIED DOWN.	A DIGITAL ROAD SIGN DISPLAYS A 'JOKE' ABOUT TRAFFIC SAFETY.
SOMEONE AT THE GAS STATION IS LITERALLY WEARING PAJAMAS.	ANOTHER CAR'S BLINKER IS LEFT ON FOR MILES.	A VEHICLE PLASTERED IN NONSENSICAL BUMPER STICKERS IS SPOTTED.	A SLOW CAR STARTS TO SPEED UP THE MOMENT THAT SOMEONE TRIES TO PASS.	A BUNCH OF OLD-TIMEY CARS APPEAR OUT OF NOWHERE ON THE HIGHWAY.
THERE'S A WESTERN WEAR STORE—NOT EVEN CLOSE TO THE ACTUAL WEST.	MALE GENITALIA IS FEATURED AS 'DECOR' ON THE BACK OF A TRUCK.	✖	A ROADSIDE FRUIT STAND IS SELLING QUESTIONABLE PRODUCE.	A TRUCK STOP HAS ITS OWN EATING CHALLENGE FOR A FREE T-SHIRT.
BATHROOMS AT THE GAS STATION ARE TOO GROSS TO USE.	AN ACTUAL TUMBLEWEED BLOWS ACROSS THE ROAD.	EVERYONE SUDDENLY STARTS GOING THE SPEED LIMIT BECAUSE OF A COP.	THE RADIO STATION JUST TURNS INTO STATIC.	THERE'S A CAR WITH A SET OF EYELASHES ON THE HEADLIGHTS.
AN 'ADULT SUPERSTORE' IS LOCATED RIGHT BESIDE A FIREWORKS SHOP.	A LANE IS CLOSED FOR REPAIRS—THAT NO ONE IS ACTUALLY WORKING ON.	SOMEONE IS WALKING ON THE SIDE OF THE HIGHWAY.	A CAR USING A TINY SPARE TIRE PASSES YOU AT 85 MPH.	A TOWN WATER TOWER IS PAINTED TO LOOK LIKE SOMETHING KITSCHY.

OBJECTIVE

OH, YOU MEAN BESIDES TRYING TO PASS THE TIME DURING THIS VACATION THAT YOU MAY OR MAY NOT HAVE EVEN WANTED TO GO ON? ISN'T THAT ENOUGH? WHAT DO YOU WANT FROM US?

WELL, WE HOPE YOU'RE AT LEAST FAMILIAR WITH THE CONCEPT OF BINGO. BECAUSE IF NOT, WELL WE ARE REALLY KIND OF WORRIED ABOUT YOU. WHAT OTHER THINGS IN LIFE HAVE YOU MISSED? SHOES? AUTOMOBILES? TWO-PLY TOILET PAPER? WE DIGRESS.

THIS VACATION BIN·GO GAME IS PLAYED MUCH LIKE THE TRADITIONAL ONE. YOUR GOAL IS TO SIMPLY BE THE FIRST TO FILL 5 SEQUENTIAL SQUARES IN A ROW, A COLUMN, OR EVEN DIAGONALLY (SEE FIGURE 1 BELOW).

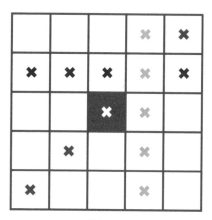

FIGURE 1

SEE THAT X IN THE CENTER SQUARE OF YOUR BOARDS? THAT'S A FREE SQUARE—WHICH MEANS EVERY PLAYER GETS THIS ONE AUTOMATICALLY. IT REALLY HELPS SO...YOU'RE WELCOME.

PLAYING THE GAME

AFTER DETERMINING HOW MANY PEOPLE ARE PLAYING, THE OWNER OF THE BOOK SHOULD PERF. OUT A CARD (OR TWO) FOR EVERYONE TO USE AS THEIR PLAY BOARD(S).

ALRIGHT, SO HERE'S HOW OUR GAME IS A BIT DIFFERENT. WE'VE PRE-FILLED EACH CARD WITH THE COMMON (YET RIDICULOUS) THINGS THAT ALWAYS SEEM TO HAPPEN WHILE TRAVELING. SO, INSTEAD OF SOMEONE JUST CALLING OUT NUMBERS, EVERYONE IS PEOPLE WATCHING INSTEAD. WHEN SOMETHING HAPPENS THAT IS ON ONE OF YOUR SQUARES, YOU CALL IT OUT (AS DISCREETLY AS APPROPRIATE, OF COURSE) AND MARK OFF THE SQUARE.

JUST REMEMBER THAT THE OTHER PLAYERS NEED TO BE AWARE OF THE 'CALL'—AND IDEALLY SEE IT AS WELL (BUT THAT'S NOT A REQUIREMENT). THAT WAY THEY CAN ALSO MARK OFF THAT SQUARE IF IT'S ON THEIR BOARD.

WINNING

WHEN A PLAYER MARKS OFF A WINNING CARD, THEY SHOULD ANNOUNCE 'BINGO.' IN THE EVENT OF A TIE, THE FIRST TO SAY IT IS THE WINNER. EITHER WAY—EVERYONE ELSE IN THE ROOM WILL PROBABLY BE WONDERING WHAT THE HELL YOU ARE DOING. ADMITTEDLY IT MIGHT BE HARD TO MAKE A TRUE BINGO, SO YOU CAN ALSO DECIDE THAT THE PLAYER WITH THE MOST SQUARES MARKED OFF IS THE WINNER.

BONUS: YOU CAN ALSO PLAY THIS AS A DRINKING GAME. IT'S SIMPLE. WHEN SOMETHING HAPPENS ON YOUR CARD, YOU HAVE TO TAKE A DRINK (AFTER TRAVELING IS DONE OF COURSE). IF YOU MAKE A BINGO—WELL NOW EVERYONE ELSE HAS TO DRINK. JUST TALLY UP DRINKS ONCE YOU'RE AT YOUR DESTINATION & GO TO THE BAR.

AIRPORT BIN×GO AIRPORT

SOMEONE IS WEARING PAJAMAS— INCLUDING SLIPPERS.	THERE'S A SHOE SHINE STAND— DESPITE IT NOT BEING 1955.	A STRANGER SITS DOWN NEXT TO YOU DESPITE ALL THE OPEN SEATING.	SOMEONE IS REPACKING A SUITCASE IN THE MIDDLE OF THE FLOOR.	THERE'S ONE SECURITY LINE OPEN FOR ABOUT 5,000 PASSENGERS.
A FAMILY OF THREE IS CARRYING ROUGHLY 23 SUITCASES.	MEMBERS OF A 'FUN' GROUP ARE ALL WEARING THE SAME SHIRT.	THERE'S AN ARGUMENT ABOUT 3 OZ. OF LIQUIDS IN SECURITY.	IMPORTANT FLIGHT UPDATES ARE COMPLETELY INAUDIBLE.	SOMEONE IS MAKING A CALL ON THE PLANE—WHILE ON SPEAKER.
AN AIRPORT EMPLOYEE NEARLY HITS SOMEONE W/ A GOLF CART.	SOMEONE IS RUNNING AT FULL SPEED TO CATCH A FLIGHT.	✖	IT TAKES AN ADULT ONE CALENDAR YEAR TO GET THEIR SHOES & BELT OFF.	THE BAR IS COMPLETELY FULL— AT 8 AM.
THE FLIGHT ATTENDANT TELLS 'JOKES' OVER THE INTERCOM.	METAL SETS OFF A METAL DETECTOR— MUCH TO THE SURPRISE OF THE TRAVELER.	SOMEONE IS USING A SUITCASE AS A PILLOW.	THERE'S SIX GENERATIONS OF BIRDS LIVING IN THE RAFTERS.	SOMEONE IS TAKING A SPONGE BATH IN THE BATHROOM.
TALKATIVE STRANGERS BECOME BEST FRIENDS AS THEY WAIT TO BOARD.	SOMEONE JUST STANDS IN THE MIDDLE OF A MOVING SIDEWALK.	THERE'S A SUSPICIOUS PUDDLE IN THE MIDDLE OF THE BATHROOM.	SOMEONE IS WEARING A FULL SUIT ON A 6 AM FLIGHT.	PASSENGERS RUSH INTO THE AISLE THE MOMENT A FLIGHT LANDS.

OBJECTIVE

OH, YOU MEAN BESIDES TRYING TO PASS THE TIME DURING THIS VACATION THAT YOU MAY OR MAY NOT HAVE EVEN WANTED TO GO ON? ISN'T THAT ENOUGH? WHAT DO YOU WANT FROM US?

WELL, WE HOPE YOU'RE AT LEAST FAMILIAR WITH THE CONCEPT OF BINGO. BECAUSE IF NOT, WELL WE ARE REALLY KIND OF WORRIED ABOUT YOU. WHAT OTHER THINGS IN LIFE HAVE YOU MISSED? SHOES? AUTOMOBILES? TWO-PLY TOILET PAPER? WE DIGRESS.

THIS VACATION BIN·GO GAME IS PLAYED MUCH LIKE THE TRADITIONAL ONE. YOUR GOAL IS TO SIMPLY BE THE FIRST TO FILL 5 SEQUENTIAL SQUARES IN A ROW, A COLUMN, OR EVEN DIAGONALLY (SEE FIGURE 1 BELOW).

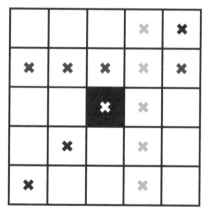

FIGURE 1

SEE THAT X IN THE CENTER SQUARE OF YOUR BOARDS? THAT'S A FREE SQUARE—WHICH MEANS EVERY PLAYER GETS THIS ONE AUTOMATICALLY. IT REALLY HELPS SO...YOU'RE WELCOME.

PLAYING THE GAME

AFTER DETERMINING HOW MANY PEOPLE ARE PLAYING, THE OWNER OF THE BOOK SHOULD PERF. OUT A CARD (OR TWO) FOR EVERYONE TO USE AS THEIR PLAY BOARD(S).

ALRIGHT, SO HERE'S HOW OUR GAME IS A BIT DIFFERENT. WE'VE PRE-FILLED EACH CARD WITH THE COMMON (YET RIDICULOUS) THINGS THAT ALWAYS SEEM TO HAPPEN WHILE TRAVELING. SO, INSTEAD OF SOMEONE JUST CALLING OUT NUMBERS, EVERYONE IS PEOPLE WATCHING INSTEAD. WHEN SOMETHING HAPPENS THAT IS ON ONE OF YOUR SQUARES, YOU CALL IT OUT (AS DISCREETLY AS APPROPRIATE, OF COURSE) AND MARK OFF THE SQUARE.

JUST REMEMBER THAT THE OTHER PLAYERS NEED TO BE AWARE OF THE 'CALL'—AND IDEALLY SEE IT AS WELL (BUT THAT'S NOT A REQUIREMENT). THAT WAY THEY CAN ALSO MARK OFF THAT SQUARE IF IT'S ON THEIR BOARD.

WINNING

WHEN A PLAYER MARKS OFF A WINNING CARD, THEY SHOULD ANNOUNCE 'BINGO.' IN THE EVENT OF A TIE, THE FIRST TO SAY IT IS THE WINNER. EITHER WAY—EVERYONE ELSE IN THE ROOM WILL PROBABLY BE WONDERING WHAT THE HELL YOU ARE DOING. ADMITTEDLY IT MIGHT BE HARD TO MAKE A TRUE BINGO, SO YOU CAN ALSO DECIDE THAT THE PLAYER WITH THE MOST SQUARES MARKED OFF IS THE WINNER.

BONUS: YOU CAN ALSO PLAY THIS AS A DRINKING GAME. IT'S SIMPLE. WHEN SOMETHING HAPPENS ON YOUR CARD, YOU HAVE TO TAKE A DRINK (AFTER TRAVELING IS DONE OF COURSE). IF YOU MAKE A BINGO—WELL NOW EVERYONE ELSE HAS TO DRINK. JUST TALLY UP DRINKS ONCE YOU'RE AT YOUR DESTINATION & GO TO THE BAR.

AIRPORT BIN×GO AIRPORT

SOMEONE IS WATCHING A MOVIE ON THEIR PHONE WITHOUT HEADPHONES.	A PASSENGER CASUALLY STROLLS THE PLANE DESPITE THE SEATBELT SIGN.	A LOUD BUSINESSMAN TALKS ABOUT BUSINESS.	A TRAVELER IS MAD THAT THEY CAN'T CARRY ON A SEDAN-SIZED DUFFEL BAG.	A PASSENGER HITS THEIR HEAD ON AN OVERHEAD BIN.
A SEX SCENE AWKWARDLY APPEARS ON A SEAT-BACK TV SCREEN.	THE 'COOL' FLIGHT ATTENDANT HANDS OUT FULL CANS OF SODA.	A PLANE SEAT IS RECLINED, REDUCING SOMEONE'S SPACE TO 3 CUBIC INCHES.	THERE IS A CRYING BABY (OR ADULT).	THERE IS A 'SERVICE ANIMAL' THAT IS CLEARLY NOT A SERVICE ANIMAL.
ONLY 1 IN EVERY 5 SELF CHECK-IN MACHINES ARE ACTUALLY WORKING.	MOST OF THE SEATS IN THE WAITING AREA ARE TAKEN BY BAGS INSTEAD OF PEOPLE.	✖	A BAG ON THE CAROUSEL IS WIDE OPEN & SPILLING EVERYWHERE.	SOMEONE BUYS LIQUOR ON THE PLANE BEFORE IT'S 9 AM.
A TRAVELER MISTAKINGLY WAITS 1 HR IN A PRECHECK LINE—ONLY TO BE REJECTED.	EVERY SINGLE PERSON IN THE AIRPORT IS SEEMINGLY IN LINE FOR COFFEE.	THERE'S A YOUTH SPORTS TEAM—WITH ROUGHLY 1,000 BAGS OF EQUIPMENT.	SOMEONE FALLS ASLEEP ON A STRANGER'S SHOULDER.	THE BEVERAGE CART SLAMS INTO THE ELBOW OF A PASSENGER.
A PASSENGER THROWS UP ON THE PLANE. REPEATEDLY.	THE SHUTTLE BUS WITHOUT SEATBELTS IS DRIVEN LIKE A FORMULA ONE RACE CAR.	SOMEONE TAKES THEIR SHOES OFF WHILE ON THE PLANE.	THERE'S NO MORE SOAP IN THE RESTROOM—IF THERE WAS ANY TO BEGIN WITH.	AT THE GIFT SHOP, A BAG OF CHIPS AND A WATER COSTS $87.

OBJECTIVE

OH, YOU MEAN BESIDES TRYING TO PASS THE TIME DURING THIS VACATION THAT YOU MAY OR MAY NOT HAVE EVEN WANTED TO GO ON? ISN'T THAT ENOUGH? WHAT DO YOU WANT FROM US?

WELL, WE HOPE YOU'RE AT LEAST FAMILIAR WITH THE CONCEPT OF BINGO. BECAUSE IF NOT, WELL WE ARE REALLY KIND OF WORRIED ABOUT YOU. WHAT OTHER THINGS IN LIFE HAVE YOU MISSED? SHOES? AUTOMOBILES? TWO-PLY TOILET PAPER? WE DIGRESS.

THIS VACATION BIN·GO GAME IS PLAYED MUCH LIKE THE TRADITIONAL ONE. YOUR GOAL IS TO SIMPLY BE THE FIRST TO FILL 5 SEQUENTIAL SQUARES IN A ROW, A COLUMN, OR EVEN DIAGONALLY (SEE FIGURE 1 BELOW).

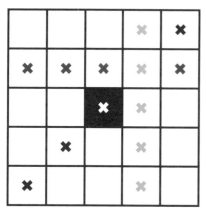

FIGURE 1

SEE THAT X IN THE CENTER SQUARE OF YOUR BOARDS? THAT'S A FREE SQUARE—WHICH MEANS EVERY PLAYER GETS THIS ONE AUTOMATICALLY. IT REALLY HELPS SO...YOU'RE WELCOME.

PLAYING THE GAME

AFTER DETERMINING HOW MANY PEOPLE ARE PLAYING, THE OWNER OF THE BOOK SHOULD PERF. OUT A CARD (OR TWO) FOR EVERYONE TO USE AS THEIR PLAY BOARD(S).

ALRIGHT, SO HERE'S HOW OUR GAME IS A BIT DIFFERENT. WE'VE PRE-FILLED EACH CARD WITH THE COMMON (YET RIDICULOUS) THINGS THAT ALWAYS SEEM TO HAPPEN WHILE TRAVELING. SO, INSTEAD OF SOMEONE JUST CALLING OUT NUMBERS, EVERYONE IS PEOPLE WATCHING INSTEAD. WHEN SOMETHING HAPPENS THAT IS ON ONE OF YOUR SQUARES, YOU CALL IT OUT (AS DISCREETLY AS APPROPRIATE, OF COURSE) AND MARK OFF THE SQUARE.

JUST REMEMBER THAT THE OTHER PLAYERS NEED TO BE AWARE OF THE 'CALL'—AND IDEALLY SEE IT AS WELL (BUT THAT'S NOT A REQUIREMENT). THAT WAY THEY CAN ALSO MARK OFF THAT SQUARE IF IT'S ON THEIR BOARD.

WINNING

WHEN A PLAYER MARKS OFF A WINNING CARD, THEY SHOULD ANNOUNCE 'BINGO.' IN THE EVENT OF A TIE, THE FIRST TO SAY IT IS THE WINNER. EITHER WAY—EVERYONE ELSE IN THE ROOM WILL PROBABLY BE WONDERING WHAT THE HELL YOU ARE DOING. ADMITTEDLY IT MIGHT BE HARD TO MAKE A TRUE BINGO, SO YOU CAN ALSO DECIDE THAT THE PLAYER WITH THE MOST SQUARES MARKED OFF IS THE WINNER.

BONUS: YOU CAN ALSO PLAY THIS AS A DRINKING GAME. IT'S SIMPLE. WHEN SOMETHING HAPPENS ON YOUR CARD, YOU HAVE TO TAKE A DRINK (AFTER TRAVELING IS DONE OF COURSE). IF YOU MAKE A BINGO—WELL NOW EVERYONE ELSE HAS TO DRINK. JUST TALLY UP DRINKS ONCE YOU'RE AT YOUR DESTINATION & GO TO THE BAR.

AIRPORT BIN×GO AIRPORT

A PASSENGER CASUALLY STROLLS THE PLANE DESPITE THE SEATBELT SIGN.	SOMEONE TAKES THEIR SHOES OFF WHILE ON THE PLANE.	MEMBERS OF A 'FUN' GROUP ARE ALL WEARING THE SAME SHIRT.	AN AIRPORT EMPLOYEE NEARLY HITS SOMEONE W/ A GOLF CART.	A TRAVELER MISTAKINGLY WAITS 1 HR IN A PRECHECK LINE—ONLY TO BE REJECTED.
SOMEONE IS WATCHING A MOVIE ON THEIR PHONE WITHOUT HEADPHONES.	SOMEONE IS REPACKING A SUITCASE IN THE MIDDLE OF THE FLOOR.	SOMEONE IS MAKING A CALL ON THE PLANE—WHILE ON SPEAKER.	SOMEONE IS RUNNING AT FULL SPEED TO CATCH A FLIGHT.	THERE'S NO MORE SOAP IN THE RESTROOM—IF THERE WAS ANY TO BEGIN WITH.
IMPORTANT FLIGHT UPDATES ARE COMPLETELY INAUDIBLE.	THERE'S ONE SECURITY LINE OPEN FOR ABOUT 5,000 PASSENGERS.	✖	THERE IS A CRYING BABY (OR ADULT).	A PASSENGER HITS THEIR HEAD ON AN OVERHEAD BIN.
EVERY SINGLE PERSON IN THE AIRPORT IS SEEMINGLY IN LINE FOR COFFEE.	A PLANE SEAT IS RECLINED, REDUCING SOMEONE'S SPACE TO 3 CUBIC INCHES.	AT THE GIFT SHOP, A BAG OF CHIPS AND A WATER COSTS $87.	THE FLIGHT ATTENDANT TELLS 'JOKES' OVER THE INTERCOM.	METAL SETS OFF A METAL DETECTOR—MUCH TO THE SURPRISE OF THE TRAVELER.
MOST OF THE SEATS IN THE WAITING AREA ARE TAKEN BY BAGS INSTEAD OF PEOPLE.	ONLY 1 IN EVERY 5 SELF CHECK-IN MACHINES ARE ACTUALLY WORKING.	THERE'S SIX GENERATIONS OF BIRDS LIVING IN THE RAFTERS.	SOMEONE IS TAKING A SPONGE BATH IN THE BATHROOM.	A LOUD BUSINESSMAN TALKS ABOUT BUSINESS.

OBJECTIVE

OH, YOU MEAN BESIDES TRYING TO PASS THE TIME DURING THIS VACATION THAT YOU MAY OR MAY NOT HAVE EVEN WANTED TO GO ON? ISN'T THAT ENOUGH? WHAT DO YOU WANT FROM US?

WELL, WE HOPE YOU'RE AT LEAST FAMILIAR WITH THE CONCEPT OF BINGO. BECAUSE IF NOT, WELL WE ARE REALLY KIND OF WORRIED ABOUT YOU. WHAT OTHER THINGS IN LIFE HAVE YOU MISSED? SHOES? AUTOMOBILES? TWO-PLY TOILET PAPER? WE DIGRESS.

THIS VACATION BIN·GO GAME IS PLAYED MUCH LIKE THE TRADITIONAL ONE. YOUR GOAL IS TO SIMPLY BE THE FIRST TO FILL 5 SEQUENTIAL SQUARES IN A ROW, A COLUMN, OR EVEN DIAGONALLY (SEE FIGURE 1 BELOW).

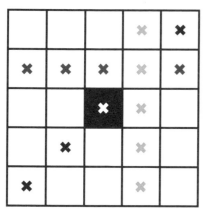

FIGURE 1

SEE THAT X IN THE CENTER SQUARE OF YOUR BOARDS? THAT'S A FREE SQUARE—WHICH MEANS EVERY PLAYER GETS THIS ONE AUTOMATICALLY. IT REALLY HELPS SO...YOU'RE WELCOME.

PLAYING THE GAME

AFTER DETERMINING HOW MANY PEOPLE ARE PLAYING, THE OWNER OF THE BOOK SHOULD PERF. OUT A CARD (OR TWO) FOR EVERYONE TO USE AS THEIR PLAY BOARD(S).

ALRIGHT, SO HERE'S HOW OUR GAME IS A BIT DIFFERENT. WE'VE PRE-FILLED EACH CARD WITH THE COMMON (YET RIDICULOUS) THINGS THAT ALWAYS SEEM TO HAPPEN WHILE TRAVELING. SO, INSTEAD OF SOMEONE JUST CALLING OUT NUMBERS, EVERYONE IS PEOPLE WATCHING INSTEAD. WHEN SOMETHING HAPPENS THAT IS ON ONE OF YOUR SQUARES, YOU CALL IT OUT (AS DISCREETLY AS APPROPRIATE, OF COURSE) AND MARK OFF THE SQUARE.

JUST REMEMBER THAT THE OTHER PLAYERS NEED TO BE AWARE OF THE 'CALL'—AND IDEALLY SEE IT AS WELL (BUT THAT'S NOT A REQUIREMENT). THAT WAY THEY CAN ALSO MARK OFF THAT SQUARE IF IT'S ON THEIR BOARD.

WINNING

WHEN A PLAYER MARKS OFF A WINNING CARD, THEY SHOULD ANNOUNCE 'BINGO.' IN THE EVENT OF A TIE, THE FIRST TO SAY IT IS THE WINNER. EITHER WAY—EVERYONE ELSE IN THE ROOM WILL PROBABLY BE WONDERING WHAT THE HELL YOU ARE DOING. ADMITTEDLY IT MIGHT BE HARD TO MAKE A TRUE BINGO, SO YOU CAN ALSO DECIDE THAT THE PLAYER WITH THE MOST SQUARES MARKED OFF IS THE WINNER.

BONUS: YOU CAN ALSO PLAY THIS AS A DRINKING GAME. IT'S SIMPLE. WHEN SOMETHING HAPPENS ON YOUR CARD, YOU HAVE TO TAKE A DRINK (AFTER TRAVELING IS DONE OF COURSE). IF YOU MAKE A BINGO—WELL NOW EVERYONE ELSE HAS TO DRINK. JUST TALLY UP DRINKS ONCE YOU'RE AT YOUR DESTINATION & GO TO THE BAR.

AIRPORT BIN×GO AIRPORT

THE BAR IS COMPLETELY FULL— AT 8 AM.	A SEX SCENE AWKWARDLY APPEARS ON A SEAT-BACK TV SCREEN.	SOMEONE JUST STANDS IN THE MIDDLE OF A MOVING SIDEWALK.	MEMBERS OF A 'FUN' GROUP ARE ALL WEARING THE SAME SHIRT.	AT THE GIFT SHOP, A BAG OF CHIPS AND A WATER COSTS $87.
A PASSENGER THROWS UP ON THE PLANE. REPEATEDLY.	EVERY SINGLE PERSON IN THE AIRPORT IS SEEMINGLY IN LINE FOR COFFEE.	THERE'S A YOUTH SPORTS TEAM—WITH ROUGHLY 1,000 BAGS OF EQUIPMENT.	SOMEONE IS USING A SUITCASE AS A PILLOW.	SOMEONE IS WEARING PAJAMAS— INCLUDING SLIPPERS.
THERE'S AN ARGUMENT ABOUT 3 OZ. OF LIQUIDS IN SECURITY.	METAL SETS OFF A METAL DETECTOR— MUCH TO THE SURPRISE OF THE TRAVELER.	✖	A TRAVELER IS MAD THAT THEY CAN'T CARRY ON A SEDAN-SIZED DUFFEL BAG.	SOMEONE IS WATCHING A MOVIE ON THEIR PHONE WITHOUT HEADPHONES.
IT TAKES AN ADULT ONE CALENDAR YEAR TO GET THEIR SHOES & BELT OFF.	A STRANGER SITS DOWN NEXT TO YOU DESPITE ALL THE OPEN SEATING.	THE SHUTTLE BUS WITHOUT SEATBELTS IS DRIVEN LIKE A FORMULA ONE RACE CAR.	A BAG ON THE CAROUSEL IS WIDE OPEN & SPILLING EVERYWHERE.	THE BEVERAGE CART SLAMS INTO THE ELBOW OF A PASSENGER.
A LOUD BUSINESSMAN TALKS ABOUT BUSINESS.	SOMEONE BUYS LIQUOR ON THE PLANE BEFORE IT'S 9 AM.	MOST OF THE SEATS IN THE WAITING AREA ARE TAKEN BY BAGS INSTEAD OF PEOPLE.	THERE'S A SUSPICIOUS PUDDLE IN THE MIDDLE OF THE BATHROOM.	THE 'COOL' FLIGHT ATTENDANT HANDS OUT FULL CANS OF SODA.

OBJECTIVE

OH, YOU MEAN BESIDES TRYING TO PASS THE
TIME DURING THIS VACATION THAT YOU MAY OR
MAY NOT HAVE EVEN WANTED TO GO ON? ISN'T
THAT ENOUGH? WHAT DO YOU WANT FROM US?

WELL, WE HOPE YOU'RE AT LEAST FAMILIAR WITH
THE CONCEPT OF BINGO. BECAUSE IF NOT, WELL
WE ARE REALLY KIND OF WORRIED ABOUT YOU.
WHAT OTHER THINGS IN LIFE HAVE YOU MISSED?
SHOES? AUTOMOBILES? TWO-PLY TOILET PAPER?
WE DIGRESS.

THIS VACATION BIN×GO GAME IS PLAYED MUCH
LIKE THE TRADITIONAL ONE. YOUR GOAL IS TO
SIMPLY BE THE FIRST TO FILL 5 SEQUENTIAL
SQUARES IN A ROW, A COLUMN, OR EVEN
DIAGONALLY (SEE FIGURE 1 BELOW).

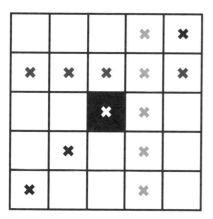

FIGURE 1

SEE THAT X IN THE CENTER SQUARE OF YOUR
BOARDS? THAT'S A FREE SQUARE—WHICH MEANS
EVERY PLAYER GETS THIS ONE AUTOMATICALLY.
IT REALLY HELPS SO...YOU'RE WELCOME.

PLAYING THE GAME

AFTER DETERMINING HOW MANY PEOPLE ARE
PLAYING, THE OWNER OF THE BOOK SHOULD
PERF. OUT A CARD (OR TWO) FOR EVERYONE TO
USE AS THEIR PLAY BOARD(S).

ALRIGHT, SO HERE'S HOW OUR GAME IS A BIT
DIFFERENT. WE'VE PRE-FILLED EACH CARD WITH
THE COMMON (YET RIDICULOUS) THINGS THAT
ALWAYS SEEM TO HAPPEN WHILE TRAVELING.
SO, INSTEAD OF SOMEONE JUST CALLING OUT
NUMBERS, EVERYONE IS PEOPLE WATCHING
INSTEAD. WHEN SOMETHING HAPPENS THAT IS
ON ONE OF YOUR SQUARES, YOU CALL IT OUT
(AS DISCREETLY AS APPROPRIATE, OF COURSE)
AND MARK OFF THE SQUARE.

JUST REMEMBER THAT THE OTHER PLAYERS NEED
TO BE AWARE OF THE 'CALL'—AND IDEALLY SEE
IT AS WELL (BUT THAT'S NOT A REQUIREMENT).
THAT WAY THEY CAN ALSO MARK OFF THAT
SQUARE IF IT'S ON THEIR BOARD.

WINNING

WHEN A PLAYER MARKS OFF A WINNING CARD,
THEY SHOULD ANNOUNCE 'BINGO.' IN THE EVENT
OF A TIE, THE FIRST TO SAY IT IS THE WINNER.
EITHER WAY—EVERYONE ELSE IN THE ROOM WILL
PROBABLY BE WONDERING WHAT THE HELL YOU
ARE DOING. ADMITTEDLY IT MIGHT BE HARD TO
MAKE A TRUE BINGO, SO YOU CAN ALSO DECIDE
THAT THE PLAYER WITH THE MOST SQUARES
MARKED OFF IS THE WINNER.

BONUS: YOU CAN ALSO PLAY THIS AS A DRINKING
GAME. IT'S SIMPLE. WHEN SOMETHING HAPPENS
ON YOUR CARD, YOU HAVE TO TAKE A DRINK
(AFTER TRAVELING IS DONE OF COURSE). IF
YOU MAKE A BINGO—WELL NOW EVERYONE ELSE
HAS TO DRINK. JUST TALLY UP DRINKS ONCE
YOU'RE AT YOUR DESTINATION & GO TO THE BAR.

AIRPORT BIN×GO AIRPORT

THERE'S AN ARGUMENT ABOUT 3 OZ. OF LIQUIDS IN SECURITY.	SOMEONE FALLS ASLEEP ON A STRANGER'S SHOULDER.	A BAG ON THE CAROUSEL IS WIDE OPEN & SPILLING EVERYWHERE.	SOMEONE IS WATCHING A MOVIE ON THEIR PHONE WITHOUT HEADPHONES.	THERE'S ONE SECURITY LINE OPEN FOR ABOUT 5,000 PASSENGERS.
IMPORTANT FLIGHT UPDATES ARE COMPLETELY INAUDIBLE.	SOMEONE IS MAKING A CALL ON THE PLANE—WHILE ON SPEAKER.	A PASSENGER THROWS UP ON THE PLANE. REPEATEDLY.	THE BAR IS COMPLETELY FULL— AT 8 AM.	SOMEONE IS REPACKING A SUITCASE IN THE MIDDLE OF THE FLOOR.
A FAMILY OF THREE IS CARRYING ROUGHLY 23 SUITCASES.	MOST OF THE SEATS IN THE WAITING AREA ARE TAKEN BY BAGS INSTEAD OF PEOPLE.	✖	SOMEONE TAKES THEIR SHOES OFF WHILE ON THE PLANE.	SOMEONE IS WEARING PAJAMAS— INCLUDING SLIPPERS.
PASSENGERS RUSH INTO THE AISLE THE MOMENT A FLIGHT LANDS.	THERE'S A YOUTH SPORTS TEAM—WITH ROUGHLY 1,000 BAGS OF EQUIPMENT.	THE 'COOL' FLIGHT ATTENDANT HANDS OUT FULL CANS OF SODA.	SOMEONE IS USING A SUITCASE AS A PILLOW.	THE BEVERAGE CART SLAMS INTO THE ELBOW OF A PASSENGER.
SOMEONE IS TAKING A SPONGE BATH IN THE BATHROOM.	SOMEONE JUST STANDS IN THE MIDDLE OF A MOVING SIDEWALK.	THERE'S NO MORE SOAP IN THE RESTROOM— IF THERE WAS ANY TO BEGIN WITH.	A PLANE SEAT IS RECLINED, REDUCING SOMEONE'S SPACE TO 3 CUBIC INCHES.	A TRAVELER MISTAKINGLY WAITS 1 HR IN A PRECHECK LINE—ONLY TO BE REJECTED.

OBJECTIVE

OH, YOU MEAN BESIDES TRYING TO PASS THE TIME DURING THIS VACATION THAT YOU MAY OR MAY NOT HAVE EVEN WANTED TO GO ON? ISN'T THAT ENOUGH? WHAT DO YOU WANT FROM US?

WELL, WE HOPE YOU'RE AT LEAST FAMILIAR WITH THE CONCEPT OF BINGO. BECAUSE IF NOT, WELL WE ARE REALLY KIND OF WORRIED ABOUT YOU. WHAT OTHER THINGS IN LIFE HAVE YOU MISSED? SHOES? AUTOMOBILES? TWO-PLY TOILET PAPER? WE DIGRESS.

THIS VACATION BIN·GO GAME IS PLAYED MUCH LIKE THE TRADITIONAL ONE. YOUR GOAL IS TO SIMPLY BE THE FIRST TO FILL 5 SEQUENTIAL SQUARES IN A ROW, A COLUMN, OR EVEN DIAGONALLY (SEE FIGURE 1 BELOW).

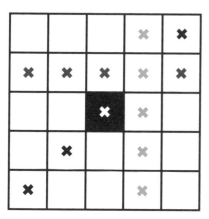

FIGURE 1

SEE THAT X IN THE CENTER SQUARE OF YOUR BOARDS? THAT'S A FREE SQUARE—WHICH MEANS EVERY PLAYER GETS THIS ONE AUTOMATICALLY. IT REALLY HELPS SO...YOU'RE WELCOME.

PLAYING THE GAME

AFTER DETERMINING HOW MANY PEOPLE ARE PLAYING, THE OWNER OF THE BOOK SHOULD PERF. OUT A CARD (OR TWO) FOR EVERYONE TO USE AS THEIR PLAY BOARD(S).

ALRIGHT, SO HERE'S HOW OUR GAME IS A BIT DIFFERENT. WE'VE PRE-FILLED EACH CARD WITH THE COMMON (YET RIDICULOUS) THINGS THAT ALWAYS SEEM TO HAPPEN WHILE TRAVELING. SO, INSTEAD OF SOMEONE JUST CALLING OUT NUMBERS, EVERYONE IS PEOPLE WATCHING INSTEAD. WHEN SOMETHING HAPPENS THAT IS ON ONE OF YOUR SQUARES, YOU CALL IT OUT (AS DISCREETLY AS APPROPRIATE, OF COURSE) AND MARK OFF THE SQUARE.

JUST REMEMBER THAT THE OTHER PLAYERS NEED TO BE AWARE OF THE 'CALL'—AND IDEALLY SEE IT AS WELL (BUT THAT'S NOT A REQUIREMENT). THAT WAY THEY CAN ALSO MARK OFF THAT SQUARE IF IT'S ON THEIR BOARD.

WINNING

WHEN A PLAYER MARKS OFF A WINNING CARD, THEY SHOULD ANNOUNCE 'BINGO.' IN THE EVENT OF A TIE, THE FIRST TO SAY IT IS THE WINNER. EITHER WAY—EVERYONE ELSE IN THE ROOM WILL PROBABLY BE WONDERING WHAT THE HELL YOU ARE DOING. ADMITTEDLY IT MIGHT BE HARD TO MAKE A TRUE BINGO, SO YOU CAN ALSO DECIDE THAT THE PLAYER WITH THE MOST SQUARES MARKED OFF IS THE WINNER.

BONUS: YOU CAN ALSO PLAY THIS AS A DRINKING GAME. IT'S SIMPLE. WHEN SOMETHING HAPPENS ON YOUR CARD, YOU HAVE TO TAKE A DRINK (AFTER TRAVELING IS DONE OF COURSE). IF YOU MAKE A BINGO—WELL NOW EVERYONE ELSE HAS TO DRINK. JUST TALLY UP DRINKS ONCE YOU'RE AT YOUR DESTINATION & GO TO THE BAR.

AIRPORT BIN×GO AIRPORT

EVERY SINGLE PERSON IN THE AIRPORT IS SEEMINGLY IN LINE FOR COFFEE.	SOMEONE IS MAKING A CALL ON THE PLANE—WHILE ON SPEAKER.	THERE'S A YOUTH SPORTS TEAM—WITH ROUGHLY 1,000 BAGS OF EQUIPMENT	SOMEONE IS WATCHING A MOVIE ON THEIR PHONE WITHOUT HEADPHONES.	THERE'S ONE SECURITY LINE OPEN FOR ABOUT 5,000 PASSENGERS.
SOMEONE IS RUNNING AT FULL SPEED TO CATCH A FLIGHT.	A PASSENGER HITS THEIR HEAD ON AN OVERHEAD BIN.	THE SHUTTLE BUS WITHOUT SEATBELTS IS DRIVEN LIKE A FORMULA ONE RACE CAR.	SOMEONE IS REPACKING A SUITCASE IN THE MIDDLE OF THE FLOOR.	A PLANE SEAT IS RECLINED, REDUCING SOMEONE'S SPACE TO 3 CUBIC INCHES.
TALKATIVE STRANGERS BECOME BEST FRIENDS AS THEY WAIT TO BOARD.	THE BAR IS COMPLETELY FULL— AT 8 AM.	✖	ONLY 1 IN EVERY 5 SELF CHECK-IN MACHINES ARE ACTUALLY WORKING.	SOMEONE TAKES THEIR SHOES OFF WHILE ON THE PLANE.
THERE'S SIX GENERATIONS OF BIRDS LIVING IN THE RAFTERS.	THE FLIGHT ATTENDANT TELLS 'JOKES' OVER THE INTERCOM.	AN AIRPORT EMPLOYEE NEARLY HITS SOMEONE W/ A GOLF CART.	MEMBERS OF A 'FUN' GROUP ARE ALL WEARING THE SAME SHIRT.	THERE IS A 'SERVICE ANIMAL' THAT IS CLEARLY NOT A SERVICE ANIMAL.
THERE'S NO MORE SOAP IN THE RESTROOM— IF THERE WAS ANY TO BEGIN WITH.	SOMEONE BUYS LIQUOR ON THE PLANE BEFORE IT'S 9 AM.	A LOUD BUSINESSMAN TALKS ABOUT BUSINESS.	THERE'S A SUSPICIOUS PUDDLE IN THE MIDDLE OF THE BATHROOM.	SOMEONE FALLS ASLEEP ON A STRANGER'S SHOULDER.

OBJECTIVE

OH, YOU MEAN BESIDES TRYING TO PASS THE TIME DURING THIS VACATION THAT YOU MAY OR MAY NOT HAVE EVEN WANTED TO GO ON? ISN'T THAT ENOUGH? WHAT DO YOU WANT FROM US?

WELL, WE HOPE YOU'RE AT LEAST FAMILIAR WITH THE CONCEPT OF BINGO. BECAUSE IF NOT, WELL WE ARE REALLY KIND OF WORRIED ABOUT YOU. WHAT OTHER THINGS IN LIFE HAVE YOU MISSED? SHOES? AUTOMOBILES? TWO-PLY TOILET PAPER? WE DIGRESS.

THIS VACATION BIN·GO GAME IS PLAYED MUCH LIKE THE TRADITIONAL ONE. YOUR GOAL IS TO SIMPLY BE THE FIRST TO FILL 5 SEQUENTIAL SQUARES IN A ROW, A COLUMN, OR EVEN DIAGONALLY (SEE FIGURE 1 BELOW).

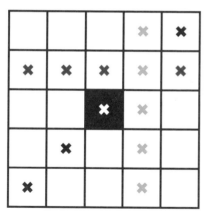

FIGURE 1

SEE THAT X IN THE CENTER SQUARE OF YOUR BOARDS? THAT'S A FREE SQUARE—WHICH MEANS EVERY PLAYER GETS THIS ONE AUTOMATICALLY. IT REALLY HELPS SO...YOU'RE WELCOME.

PLAYING THE GAME

AFTER DETERMINING HOW MANY PEOPLE ARE PLAYING, THE OWNER OF THE BOOK SHOULD PERF. OUT A CARD (OR TWO) FOR EVERYONE TO USE AS THEIR PLAY BOARD(S).

ALRIGHT, SO HERE'S HOW OUR GAME IS A BIT DIFFERENT. WE'VE PRE-FILLED EACH CARD WITH THE COMMON (YET RIDICULOUS) THINGS THAT ALWAYS SEEM TO HAPPEN WHILE TRAVELING. SO, INSTEAD OF SOMEONE JUST CALLING OUT NUMBERS, EVERYONE IS PEOPLE WATCHING INSTEAD. WHEN SOMETHING HAPPENS THAT IS ON ONE OF YOUR SQUARES, YOU CALL IT OUT (AS DISCREETLY AS APPROPRIATE, OF COURSE) AND MARK OFF THE SQUARE.

JUST REMEMBER THAT THE OTHER PLAYERS NEED TO BE AWARE OF THE 'CALL'—AND IDEALLY SEE IT AS WELL (BUT THAT'S NOT A REQUIREMENT). THAT WAY THEY CAN ALSO MARK OFF THAT SQUARE IF IT'S ON THEIR BOARD.

WINNING

WHEN A PLAYER MARKS OFF A WINNING CARD, THEY SHOULD ANNOUNCE 'BINGO.' IN THE EVENT OF A TIE, THE FIRST TO SAY IT IS THE WINNER. EITHER WAY—EVERYONE ELSE IN THE ROOM WILL PROBABLY BE WONDERING WHAT THE HELL YOU ARE DOING. ADMITTEDLY IT MIGHT BE HARD TO MAKE A TRUE BINGO, SO YOU CAN ALSO DECIDE THAT THE PLAYER WITH THE MOST SQUARES MARKED OFF IS THE WINNER.

BONUS: YOU CAN ALSO PLAY THIS AS A DRINKING GAME. IT'S SIMPLE. WHEN SOMETHING HAPPENS ON YOUR CARD, YOU HAVE TO TAKE A DRINK (AFTER TRAVELING IS DONE OF COURSE). IF YOU MAKE A BINGO—WELL NOW EVERYONE ELSE HAS TO DRINK. JUST TALLY UP DRINKS ONCE YOU'RE AT YOUR DESTINATION & GO TO THE BAR.

AIRPORT BIN×GO AIRPORT

THERE'S SIX GENERATIONS OF BIRDS LIVING IN THE RAFTERS.	TALKATIVE STRANGERS BECOME BEST FRIENDS AS THEY WAIT TO BOARD.	A PASSENGER HITS THEIR HEAD ON AN OVERHEAD BIN.	THE BAR IS COMPLETELY FULL— AT 8 AM.	THE 'COOL' FLIGHT ATTENDANT HANDS OUT FULL CANS OF SODA.
THE SHUTTLE BUS WITHOUT SEATBELTS IS DRIVEN LIKE A FORMULA ONE RACE CAR.	SOMEONE IS MAKING A CALL ON THE PLANE—WHILE ON SPEAKER.	A SEX SCENE AWKWARDLY APPEARS ON A SEAT-BACK TV SCREEN.	A TRAVELER IS MAD THAT THEY CAN'T CARRY ON A SEDAN-SIZED DUFFEL BAG.	THERE'S A YOUTH SPORTS TEAM—WITH ROUGHLY 1,000 BAGS OF EQUIPMENT.
A BAG ON THE CAROUSEL IS WIDE OPEN & SPILLING EVERYWHERE.	SOMEONE IS RUNNING AT FULL SPEED TO CATCH A FLIGHT.	✖	A LOUD BUSINESSMAN TALKS ABOUT BUSINESS.	THERE'S NO MORE SOAP IN THE RESTROOM— IF THERE WAS ANY TO BEGIN WITH.
THERE IS A 'SERVICE ANIMAL' THAT IS CLEARLY NOT A SERVICE ANIMAL.	A PASSENGER CASUALLY STROLLS THE PLANE DESPITE THE SEATBELT SIGN.	AT THE GIFT SHOP, A BAG OF CHIPS AND A WATER COSTS $87.	THERE'S A SUSPICIOUS PUDDLE IN THE MIDDLE OF THE BATHROOM.	A FAMILY OF THREE IS CARRYING ROUGHLY 23 SUITCASES.
A TRAVELER MISTAKINGLY WAITS 1 HR IN A PRECHECK LINE—ONLY TO BE REJECTED.	SOMEONE IS WEARING A FULL SUIT ON A 6 AM FLIGHT.	SOMEONE IS WATCHING A MOVIE ON THEIR PHONE WITHOUT HEADPHONES.	THE FLIGHT ATTENDANT TELLS 'JOKES' OVER THE INTERCOM.	A STRANGER SITS DOWN NEXT TO YOU DESPITE ALL THE OPEN SEATING.

HOW TO PLAY BIN×GO HOW TO PLAY

OBJECTIVE

OH, YOU MEAN BESIDES TRYING TO PASS THE
TIME DURING THIS VACATION THAT YOU MAY OR
MAY NOT HAVE EVEN WANTED TO GO ON? ISN'T
THAT ENOUGH? WHAT DO YOU WANT FROM US?

WELL, WE HOPE YOU'RE AT LEAST FAMILIAR WITH
THE CONCEPT OF BINGO. BECAUSE IF NOT, WELL
WE ARE REALLY KIND OF WORRIED ABOUT YOU.
WHAT OTHER THINGS IN LIFE HAVE YOU MISSED?
SHOES? AUTOMOBILES? TWO-PLY TOILET PAPER?
WE DIGRESS.

THIS VACATION BIN·GO GAME IS PLAYED MUCH
LIKE THE TRADITIONAL ONE. YOUR GOAL IS TO
SIMPLY BE THE FIRST TO FILL 5 SEQUENTIAL
SQUARES IN A ROW, A COLUMN, OR EVEN
DIAGONALLY (SEE FIGURE 1 BELOW).

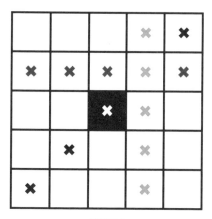

FIGURE 1

SEE THAT X IN THE CENTER SQUARE OF YOUR
BOARDS? THAT'S A FREE SQUARE—WHICH MEANS
EVERY PLAYER GETS THIS ONE AUTOMATICALLY.
IT REALLY HELPS SO...YOU'RE WELCOME.

PLAYING THE GAME

AFTER DETERMINING HOW MANY PEOPLE ARE
PLAYING, THE OWNER OF THE BOOK SHOULD
PERF. OUT A CARD (OR TWO) FOR EVERYONE TO
USE AS THEIR PLAY BOARD(S).

ALRIGHT, SO HERE'S HOW OUR GAME IS A BIT
DIFFERENT. WE'VE PRE-FILLED EACH CARD WITH
THE COMMON (YET RIDICULOUS) THINGS THAT
ALWAYS SEEM TO HAPPEN WHILE TRAVELING.
SO, INSTEAD OF SOMEONE JUST CALLING OUT
NUMBERS, EVERYONE IS PEOPLE WATCHING
INSTEAD. WHEN SOMETHING HAPPENS THAT IS
ON ONE OF YOUR SQUARES, YOU CALL IT OUT
(AS DISCREETLY AS APPROPRIATE, OF COURSE)
AND MARK OFF THE SQUARE.

JUST REMEMBER THAT THE OTHER PLAYERS NEED
TO BE AWARE OF THE 'CALL'—AND IDEALLY SEE
IT AS WELL (BUT THAT'S NOT A REQUIREMENT).
THAT WAY THEY CAN ALSO MARK OFF THAT
SQUARE IF IT'S ON THEIR BOARD.

WINNING

WHEN A PLAYER MARKS OFF A WINNING CARD,
THEY SHOULD ANNOUNCE 'BINGO.' IN THE EVENT
OF A TIE, THE FIRST TO SAY IT IS THE WINNER.
EITHER WAY—EVERYONE ELSE IN THE ROOM WILL
PROBABLY BE WONDERING WHAT THE HELL YOU
ARE DOING. ADMITTEDLY IT MIGHT BE HARD TO
MAKE A TRUE BINGO, SO YOU CAN ALSO DECIDE
THAT THE PLAYER WITH THE MOST SQUARES
MARKED OFF IS THE WINNER.

BONUS: YOU CAN ALSO PLAY THIS AS A DRINKING
GAME. IT'S SIMPLE. WHEN SOMETHING HAPPENS
ON YOUR CARD, YOU HAVE TO TAKE A DRINK
(AFTER TRAVELING IS DONE OF COURSE). IF
YOU MAKE A BINGO—WELL NOW EVERYONE ELSE
HAS TO DRINK. JUST TALLY UP DRINKS ONCE
YOU'RE AT YOUR DESTINATION & GO TO THE BAR.

AIRPORT BIN×GO AIRPORT

SOMEONE IS WEARING A FULL SUIT ON A 6 AM FLIGHT.	A BAG ON THE CAROUSEL IS WIDE OPEN & SPILLING EVERYWHERE.	THE SHUTTLE BUS WITHOUT SEATBELTS IS DRIVEN LIKE A FORMULA ONE RACE CAR.	A TRAVELER MISTAKINGLY WAITS 1 HR IN A PRECHECK LINE—ONLY TO BE REJECTED.	A PASSENGER HITS THEIR HEAD ON AN OVERHEAD BIN.
THERE IS A CRYING BABY (OR ADULT).	SOMEONE JUST STANDS IN THE MIDDLE OF A MOVING SIDEWALK.	IT TAKES AN ADULT ONE CALENDAR YEAR TO GET THEIR SHOES & BELT OFF.	THE FLIGHT ATTENDANT TELLS 'JOKES' OVER THE INTERCOM.	A TRAVELER IS MAD THAT THEY CAN'T CARRY ON A SEDAN-SIZED DUFFEL BAG.
THERE'S ONE SECURITY LINE OPEN FOR ABOUT 5,000 PASSENGERS.	THERE'S A SHOE SHINE STAND— DESPITE IT NOT BEING 1955.	✖	THE BAR IS COMPLETELY FULL— AT 8 AM.	A PASSENGER CASUALLY STROLLS THE PLANE DESPITE THE SEATBELT SIGN.
A PLANE SEAT IS RECLINED, REDUCING SOMEONE'S SPACE TO 3 CUBIC INCHES.	METAL SETS OFF A METAL DETECTOR— MUCH TO THE SURPRISE OF THE TRAVELER.	THERE'S A YOUTH SPORTS TEAM—WITH ROUGHLY 1,000 BAGS OF EQUIPMENT	THERE IS A 'SERVICE ANIMAL' THAT IS CLEARLY NOT A SERVICE ANIMAL.	PASSENGERS RUSH INTO THE AISLE THE MOMENT A FLIGHT LANDS.
THERE'S SIX GENERATIONS OF BIRDS LIVING IN THE RAFTERS.	SOMEONE IS TAKING A SPONGE BATH IN THE BATHROOM.	TALKATIVE STRANGERS BECOME BEST FRIENDS AS THEY WAIT TO BOARD.	ONLY 1 IN EVERY 5 SELF CHECK-IN MACHINES ARE ACTUALLY WORKING.	THERE'S A SUSPICIOUS PUDDLE IN THE MIDDLE OF THE BATHROOM.

OBJECTIVE

OH, YOU MEAN BESIDES TRYING TO PASS THE TIME DURING THIS VACATION THAT YOU MAY OR MAY NOT HAVE EVEN WANTED TO GO ON? ISN'T THAT ENOUGH? WHAT DO YOU WANT FROM US?

WELL, WE HOPE YOU'RE AT LEAST FAMILIAR WITH THE CONCEPT OF BINGO. BECAUSE IF NOT, WELL WE ARE REALLY KIND OF WORRIED ABOUT YOU. WHAT OTHER THINGS IN LIFE HAVE YOU MISSED? SHOES? AUTOMOBILES? TWO-PLY TOILET PAPER? WE DIGRESS.

THIS VACATION BIN·GO GAME IS PLAYED MUCH LIKE THE TRADITIONAL ONE. YOUR GOAL IS TO SIMPLY BE THE FIRST TO FILL 5 SEQUENTIAL SQUARES IN A ROW, A COLUMN, OR EVEN DIAGONALLY (SEE FIGURE 1 BELOW).

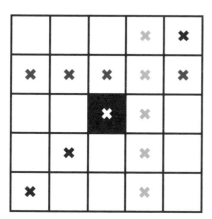

FIGURE 1

SEE THAT X IN THE CENTER SQUARE OF YOUR BOARDS? THAT'S A FREE SQUARE—WHICH MEANS EVERY PLAYER GETS THIS ONE AUTOMATICALLY. IT REALLY HELPS SO...YOU'RE WELCOME.

PLAYING THE GAME

AFTER DETERMINING HOW MANY PEOPLE ARE PLAYING, THE OWNER OF THE BOOK SHOULD PERF. OUT A CARD (OR TWO) FOR EVERYONE TO USE AS THEIR PLAY BOARD(S).

ALRIGHT, SO HERE'S HOW OUR GAME IS A BIT DIFFERENT. WE'VE PRE-FILLED EACH CARD WITH THE COMMON (YET RIDICULOUS) THINGS THAT ALWAYS SEEM TO HAPPEN WHILE TRAVELING. SO, INSTEAD OF SOMEONE JUST CALLING OUT NUMBERS, EVERYONE IS PEOPLE WATCHING INSTEAD. WHEN SOMETHING HAPPENS THAT IS ON ONE OF YOUR SQUARES, YOU CALL IT OUT (AS DISCREETLY AS APPROPRIATE, OF COURSE) AND MARK OFF THE SQUARE.

JUST REMEMBER THAT THE OTHER PLAYERS NEED TO BE AWARE OF THE 'CALL'—AND IDEALLY SEE IT AS WELL (BUT THAT'S NOT A REQUIREMENT). THAT WAY THEY CAN ALSO MARK OFF THAT SQUARE IF IT'S ON THEIR BOARD.

WINNING

WHEN A PLAYER MARKS OFF A WINNING CARD, THEY SHOULD ANNOUNCE 'BINGO.' IN THE EVENT OF A TIE, THE FIRST TO SAY IT IS THE WINNER. EITHER WAY—EVERYONE ELSE IN THE ROOM WILL PROBABLY BE WONDERING WHAT THE HELL YOU ARE DOING. ADMITTEDLY IT MIGHT BE HARD TO MAKE A TRUE BINGO, SO YOU CAN ALSO DECIDE THAT THE PLAYER WITH THE MOST SQUARES MARKED OFF IS THE WINNER.

BONUS: YOU CAN ALSO PLAY THIS AS A DRINKING GAME. IT'S SIMPLE. WHEN SOMETHING HAPPENS ON YOUR CARD, YOU HAVE TO TAKE A DRINK (AFTER TRAVELING IS DONE OF COURSE). IF YOU MAKE A BINGO—WELL NOW EVERYONE ELSE HAS TO DRINK. JUST TALLY UP DRINKS ONCE YOU'RE AT YOUR DESTINATION & GO TO THE BAR.

PASSENGERS RUSH INTO THE AISLE THE MOMENT A FLIGHT LANDS.	SOMEONE IS REPACKING A SUITCASE IN THE MIDDLE OF THE FLOOR.	METAL SETS OFF A METAL DETECTOR— MUCH TO THE SURPRISE OF THE TRAVELER.	SOMEONE JUST STANDS IN THE MIDDLE OF A MOVING SIDEWALK.	AT THE GIFT SHOP, A BAG OF CHIPS AND A WATER COSTS $87.
A PASSENGER HITS THEIR HEAD ON AN OVERHEAD BIN.	THE BEVERAGE CART SLAMS INTO THE ELBOW OF A PASSENGER.	THERE'S A YOUTH SPORTS TEAM—WITH ROUGHLY 1,000 BAGS OF EQUIPMENT	A SEX SCENE AWKWARDLY APPEARS ON A SEAT-BACK TV SCREEN.	MOST OF THE SEATS IN THE WAITING AREA ARE TAKEN BY BAGS INSTEAD OF PEOPLE.
THERE IS A CRYING BABY (OR ADULT).	SOMEONE IS USING A SUITCASE AS A PILLOW.	✖	SOMEONE IS WEARING PAJAMAS— INCLUDING SLIPPERS.	THERE IS A 'SERVICE ANIMAL' THAT IS CLEARLY NOT A SERVICE ANIMAL.
TALKATIVE STRANGERS BECOME BEST FRIENDS AS THEY WAIT TO BOARD.	THE 'COOL' FLIGHT ATTENDANT HANDS OUT FULL CANS OF SODA.	THE SHUTTLE BUS WITHOUT SEATBELTS IS DRIVEN LIKE A FORMULA ONE RACE CAR.	A LOUD BUSINESSMAN TALKS ABOUT BUSINESS.	A FAMILY OF THREE IS CARRYING ROUGHLY 23 SUITCASES.
A BAG ON THE CAROUSEL IS WIDE OPEN & SPILLING EVERYWHERE.	SOMEONE IS RUNNING AT FULL SPEED TO CATCH A FLIGHT.	MEMBERS OF A 'FUN' GROUP ARE ALL WEARING THE SAME SHIRT.	THERE'S A SHOE SHINE STAND— DESPITE IT NOT BEING 1955.	A PASSENGER CASUALLY STROLLS THE PLANE DESPITE THE SEATBELT SIGN.

OBJECTIVE

OH, YOU MEAN BESIDES TRYING TO PASS THE TIME DURING THIS VACATION THAT YOU MAY OR MAY NOT HAVE EVEN WANTED TO GO ON? ISN'T THAT ENOUGH? WHAT DO YOU WANT FROM US?

WELL, WE HOPE YOU'RE AT LEAST FAMILIAR WITH THE CONCEPT OF BINGO. BECAUSE IF NOT, WELL WE ARE REALLY KIND OF WORRIED ABOUT YOU. WHAT OTHER THINGS IN LIFE HAVE YOU MISSED? SHOES? AUTOMOBILES? TWO-PLY TOILET PAPER? WE DIGRESS.

THIS VACATION BIN·GO GAME IS PLAYED MUCH LIKE THE TRADITIONAL ONE. YOUR GOAL IS TO SIMPLY BE THE FIRST TO FILL 5 SEQUENTIAL SQUARES IN A ROW, A COLUMN, OR EVEN DIAGONALLY (SEE FIGURE 1 BELOW).

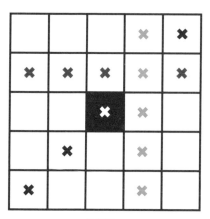

FIGURE 1

SEE THAT X IN THE CENTER SQUARE OF YOUR BOARDS? THAT'S A FREE SQUARE—WHICH MEANS EVERY PLAYER GETS THIS ONE AUTOMATICALLY. IT REALLY HELPS SO...YOU'RE WELCOME.

PLAYING THE GAME

AFTER DETERMINING HOW MANY PEOPLE ARE PLAYING, THE OWNER OF THE BOOK SHOULD PERF. OUT A CARD (OR TWO) FOR EVERYONE TO USE AS THEIR PLAY BOARD(S).

ALRIGHT, SO HERE'S HOW OUR GAME IS A BIT DIFFERENT. WE'VE PRE-FILLED EACH CARD WITH THE COMMON (YET RIDICULOUS) THINGS THAT ALWAYS SEEM TO HAPPEN WHILE TRAVELING. SO, INSTEAD OF SOMEONE JUST CALLING OUT NUMBERS, EVERYONE IS PEOPLE WATCHING INSTEAD. WHEN SOMETHING HAPPENS THAT IS ON ONE OF YOUR SQUARES, YOU CALL IT OUT (AS DISCREETLY AS APPROPRIATE, OF COURSE) AND MARK OFF THE SQUARE.

JUST REMEMBER THAT THE OTHER PLAYERS NEED TO BE AWARE OF THE 'CALL'—AND IDEALLY SEE IT AS WELL (BUT THAT'S NOT A REQUIREMENT). THAT WAY THEY CAN ALSO MARK OFF THAT SQUARE IF IT'S ON THEIR BOARD.

WINNING

WHEN A PLAYER MARKS OFF A WINNING CARD, THEY SHOULD ANNOUNCE 'BINGO.' IN THE EVENT OF A TIE, THE FIRST TO SAY IT IS THE WINNER. EITHER WAY—EVERYONE ELSE IN THE ROOM WILL PROBABLY BE WONDERING WHAT THE HELL YOU ARE DOING. ADMITTEDLY IT MIGHT BE HARD TO MAKE A TRUE BINGO, SO YOU CAN ALSO DECIDE THAT THE PLAYER WITH THE MOST SQUARES MARKED OFF IS THE WINNER.

BONUS: YOU CAN ALSO PLAY THIS AS A DRINKING GAME. IT'S SIMPLE. WHEN SOMETHING HAPPENS ON YOUR CARD, YOU HAVE TO TAKE A DRINK (AFTER TRAVELING IS DONE OF COURSE). IF YOU MAKE A BINGO—WELL NOW EVERYONE ELSE HAS TO DRINK. JUST TALLY UP DRINKS ONCE YOU'RE AT YOUR DESTINATION & GO TO THE BAR.

AIRPORT **BIN×GO** AIRPORT

THERE'S A YOUTH SPORTS TEAM—WITH ROUGHLY 1,000 BAGS OF EQUIPMENT	SOMEONE IS TAKING A SPONGE BATH IN THE BATHROOM.	PASSENGERS RUSH INTO THE AISLE THE MOMENT A FLIGHT LANDS.	AN AIRPORT EMPLOYEE NEARLY HITS SOMEONE W/ A GOLF CART.	SOMEONE TAKES THEIR SHOES OFF WHILE ON THE PLANE.
IMPORTANT FLIGHT UPDATES ARE COMPLETELY INAUDIBLE.	SOMEONE FALLS ASLEEP ON A STRANGER'S SHOULDER.	THE 'COOL' FLIGHT ATTENDANT HANDS OUT FULL CANS OF SODA.	THERE IS A 'SERVICE ANIMAL' THAT IS CLEARLY NOT A SERVICE ANIMAL.	A BAG ON THE CAROUSEL IS WIDE OPEN & SPILLING EVERYWHERE.
SOMEONE BUYS LIQUOR ON THE PLANE BEFORE IT'S 9 AM.	SOMEONE IS WEARING PAJAMAS— INCLUDING SLIPPERS.	✖	A PASSENGER THROWS UP ON THE PLANE. REPEATEDLY.	THE SHUTTLE BUS WITHOUT SEATBELTS IS DRIVEN LIKE A FORMULA ONE RACE CAR.
SOMEONE IS REPACKING A SUITCASE IN THE MIDDLE OF THE FLOOR.	THERE'S A SHOE SHINE STAND— DESPITE IT NOT BEING 1955.	SOMEONE IS WEARING A FULL SUIT ON A 6 AM FLIGHT.	THERE'S NO MORE SOAP IN THE RESTROOM— IF THERE WAS ANY TO BEGIN WITH.	A TRAVELER IS MAD THAT THEY CAN'T CARRY ON A SEDAN-SIZED DUFFEL BAG.
THERE'S AN ARGUMENT ABOUT 3 OZ. OF LIQUIDS IN SECURITY.	A PLANE SEAT IS RECLINED, REDUCING SOMEONE'S SPACE TO 3 CUBIC INCHES.	A PASSENGER CASUALLY STROLLS THE PLANE DESPITE THE SEATBELT SIGN.	IT TAKES AN ADULT ONE CALENDAR YEAR TO GET THEIR SHOES & BELT OFF.	THERE'S ONE SECURITY LINE OPEN FOR ABOUT 5,000 PASSENGERS.

OBJECTIVE

OH, YOU MEAN BESIDES TRYING TO PASS THE TIME DURING THIS VACATION THAT YOU MAY OR MAY NOT HAVE EVEN WANTED TO GO ON? ISN'T THAT ENOUGH? WHAT DO YOU WANT FROM US?

WELL, WE HOPE YOU'RE AT LEAST FAMILIAR WITH THE CONCEPT OF BINGO. BECAUSE IF NOT, WELL WE ARE REALLY KIND OF WORRIED ABOUT YOU. WHAT OTHER THINGS IN LIFE HAVE YOU MISSED? SHOES? AUTOMOBILES? TWO-PLY TOILET PAPER? WE DIGRESS.

THIS VACATION BIN·GO GAME IS PLAYED MUCH LIKE THE TRADITIONAL ONE. YOUR GOAL IS TO SIMPLY BE THE FIRST TO FILL 5 SEQUENTIAL SQUARES IN A ROW, A COLUMN, OR EVEN DIAGONALLY (SEE FIGURE 1 BELOW).

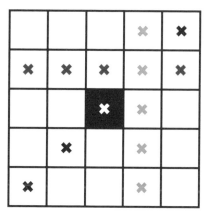

FIGURE 1

SEE THAT X IN THE CENTER SQUARE OF YOUR BOARDS? THAT'S A FREE SQUARE—WHICH MEANS EVERY PLAYER GETS THIS ONE AUTOMATICALLY. IT REALLY HELPS SO...YOU'RE WELCOME.

PLAYING THE GAME

AFTER DETERMINING HOW MANY PEOPLE ARE PLAYING, THE OWNER OF THE BOOK SHOULD PERF. OUT A CARD (OR TWO) FOR EVERYONE TO USE AS THEIR PLAY BOARD(S).

ALRIGHT, SO HERE'S HOW OUR GAME IS A BIT DIFFERENT. WE'VE PRE-FILLED EACH CARD WITH THE COMMON (YET RIDICULOUS) THINGS THAT ALWAYS SEEM TO HAPPEN WHILE TRAVELING. SO, INSTEAD OF SOMEONE JUST CALLING OUT NUMBERS, EVERYONE IS PEOPLE WATCHING INSTEAD. WHEN SOMETHING HAPPENS THAT IS ON ONE OF YOUR SQUARES, YOU CALL IT OUT (AS DISCREETLY AS APPROPRIATE, OF COURSE) AND MARK OFF THE SQUARE.

JUST REMEMBER THAT THE OTHER PLAYERS NEED TO BE AWARE OF THE 'CALL'—AND IDEALLY SEE IT AS WELL (BUT THAT'S NOT A REQUIREMENT). THAT WAY THEY CAN ALSO MARK OFF THAT SQUARE IF IT'S ON THEIR BOARD.

WINNING

WHEN A PLAYER MARKS OFF A WINNING CARD, THEY SHOULD ANNOUNCE 'BINGO.' IN THE EVENT OF A TIE, THE FIRST TO SAY IT IS THE WINNER. EITHER WAY—EVERYONE ELSE IN THE ROOM WILL PROBABLY BE WONDERING WHAT THE HELL YOU ARE DOING. ADMITTEDLY IT MIGHT BE HARD TO MAKE A TRUE BINGO, SO YOU CAN ALSO DECIDE THAT THE PLAYER WITH THE MOST SQUARES MARKED OFF IS THE WINNER.

BONUS: YOU CAN ALSO PLAY THIS AS A DRINKING GAME. IT'S SIMPLE. WHEN SOMETHING HAPPENS ON YOUR CARD, YOU HAVE TO TAKE A DRINK (AFTER TRAVELING IS DONE OF COURSE). IF YOU MAKE A BINGO—WELL NOW EVERYONE ELSE HAS TO DRINK. JUST TALLY UP DRINKS ONCE YOU'RE AT YOUR DESTINATION & GO TO THE BAR.

AIRPORT BIN×GO AIRPORT

SOMEONE IS TAKING A SPONGE BATH IN THE BATHROOM.	A STRANGER SITS DOWN NEXT TO YOU DESPITE ALL THE OPEN SEATING.	A LOUD BUSINESSMAN TALKS ABOUT BUSINESS.	IT TAKES AN ADULT ONE CALENDAR YEAR TO GET THEIR SHOES & BELT OFF.	SOMEONE TAKES THEIR SHOES OFF WHILE ON THE PLANE.
A FAMILY OF THREE IS CARRYING ROUGHLY 23 SUITCASES.	THE 'COOL' FLIGHT ATTENDANT HANDS OUT FULL CANS OF SODA.	METAL SETS OFF A METAL DETECTOR— MUCH TO THE SURPRISE OF THE TRAVELER.	A TRAVELER IS MAD THAT THEY CAN'T CARRY ON A SEDAN-SIZED DUFFEL BAG.	THERE'S A YOUTH SPORTS TEAM—WITH ROUGHLY 1,000 BAGS OF EQUIPMENT
AN AIRPORT EMPLOYEE NEARLY HITS SOMEONE W/ A GOLF CART.	THE BEVERAGE CART SLAMS INTO THE ELBOW OF A PASSENGER.	✖	A SEX SCENE AWKWARDLY APPEARS ON A SEAT-BACK TV SCREEN.	THE FLIGHT ATTENDANT TELLS 'JOKES' OVER THE INTERCOM.
TALKATIVE STRANGERS BECOME BEST FRIENDS AS THEY WAIT TO BOARD.	SOMEONE IS USING A SUITCASE AS A PILLOW.	A TRAVELER MISTAKINGLY WAITS 1 HR IN A PRECHECK LINE—ONLY TO BE REJECTED.	THERE'S ONE SECURITY LINE OPEN FOR ABOUT 5,000 PASSENGERS.	SOMEONE JUST STANDS IN THE MIDDLE OF A MOVING SIDEWALK.
MEMBERS OF A 'FUN' GROUP ARE ALL WEARING THE SAME SHIRT.	A PASSENGER HITS THEIR HEAD ON AN OVERHEAD BIN.	SOMEONE BUYS LIQUOR ON THE PLANE BEFORE IT'S 9 AM.	SOMEONE IS WEARING A FULL SUIT ON A 6 AM FLIGHT.	THERE'S A SHOE SHINE STAND— DESPITE IT NOT BEING 1955.

OBJECTIVE

OH, YOU MEAN BESIDES TRYING TO PASS THE TIME DURING THIS VACATION THAT YOU MAY OR MAY NOT HAVE EVEN WANTED TO GO ON? ISN'T THAT ENOUGH? WHAT DO YOU WANT FROM US?

WELL, WE HOPE YOU'RE AT LEAST FAMILIAR WITH THE CONCEPT OF BINGO. BECAUSE IF NOT, WELL WE ARE REALLY KIND OF WORRIED ABOUT YOU. WHAT OTHER THINGS IN LIFE HAVE YOU MISSED? SHOES? AUTOMOBILES? TWO-PLY TOILET PAPER? WE DIGRESS.

THIS VACATION BIN·GO GAME IS PLAYED MUCH LIKE THE TRADITIONAL ONE. YOUR GOAL IS TO SIMPLY BE THE FIRST TO FILL 5 SEQUENTIAL SQUARES IN A ROW, A COLUMN, OR EVEN DIAGONALLY (SEE FIGURE 1 BELOW).

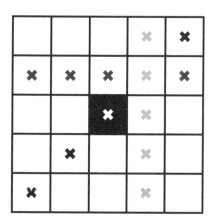

FIGURE 1

SEE THAT X IN THE CENTER SQUARE OF YOUR BOARDS? THAT'S A FREE SQUARE—WHICH MEANS EVERY PLAYER GETS THIS ONE AUTOMATICALLY. IT REALLY HELPS SO...YOU'RE WELCOME.

PLAYING THE GAME

AFTER DETERMINING HOW MANY PEOPLE ARE PLAYING, THE OWNER OF THE BOOK SHOULD PERF. OUT A CARD (OR TWO) FOR EVERYONE TO USE AS THEIR PLAY BOARD(S).

ALRIGHT, SO HERE'S HOW OUR GAME IS A BIT DIFFERENT. WE'VE PRE-FILLED EACH CARD WITH THE COMMON (YET RIDICULOUS) THINGS THAT ALWAYS SEEM TO HAPPEN WHILE TRAVELING. SO, INSTEAD OF SOMEONE JUST CALLING OUT NUMBERS, EVERYONE IS PEOPLE WATCHING INSTEAD. WHEN SOMETHING HAPPENS THAT IS ON ONE OF YOUR SQUARES, YOU CALL IT OUT (AS DISCREETLY AS APPROPRIATE, OF COURSE) AND MARK OFF THE SQUARE.

JUST REMEMBER THAT THE OTHER PLAYERS NEED TO BE AWARE OF THE 'CALL'—AND IDEALLY SEE IT AS WELL (BUT THAT'S NOT A REQUIREMENT). THAT WAY THEY CAN ALSO MARK OFF THAT SQUARE IF IT'S ON THEIR BOARD.

WINNING

WHEN A PLAYER MARKS OFF A WINNING CARD, THEY SHOULD ANNOUNCE 'BINGO.' IN THE EVENT OF A TIE, THE FIRST TO SAY IT IS THE WINNER. EITHER WAY—EVERYONE ELSE IN THE ROOM WILL PROBABLY BE WONDERING WHAT THE HELL YOU ARE DOING. ADMITTEDLY IT MIGHT BE HARD TO MAKE A TRUE BINGO, SO YOU CAN ALSO DECIDE THAT THE PLAYER WITH THE MOST SQUARES MARKED OFF IS THE WINNER.

BONUS: YOU CAN ALSO PLAY THIS AS A DRINKING GAME. IT'S SIMPLE. WHEN SOMETHING HAPPENS ON YOUR CARD, YOU HAVE TO TAKE A DRINK (AFTER TRAVELING IS DONE OF COURSE). IF YOU MAKE A BINGO—WELL NOW EVERYONE ELSE HAS TO DRINK. JUST TALLY UP DRINKS ONCE YOU'RE AT YOUR DESTINATION & GO TO THE BAR.

AIRPORT BIN×GO AIRPORT

TALKATIVE STRANGERS BECOME BEST FRIENDS AS THEY WAIT TO BOARD.	THERE'S AN ARGUMENT ABOUT 3 OZ. OF LIQUIDS IN SECURITY.	SOMEONE FALLS ASLEEP ON A STRANGER'S SHOULDER.	THERE'S A YOUTH SPORTS TEAM—WITH ROUGHLY 1,000 BAGS OF EQUIPMENT.	SOMEONE IS USING A SUITCASE AS A PILLOW.
THE FLIGHT ATTENDANT TELLS 'JOKES' OVER THE INTERCOM.	SOMEONE IS TAKING A SPONGE BATH IN THE BATHROOM.	A PASSENGER THROWS UP ON THE PLANE. REPEATEDLY.	A PLANE SEAT IS RECLINED, REDUCING SOMEONE'S SPACE TO 3 CUBIC INCHES.	IMPORTANT FLIGHT UPDATES ARE COMPLETELY INAUDIBLE.
AN AIRPORT EMPLOYEE NEARLY HITS SOMEONE W/ A GOLF CART.	SOMEONE BUYS LIQUOR ON THE PLANE BEFORE IT'S 9 AM.	✖	ONLY 1 IN EVERY 5 SELF CHECK-IN MACHINES ARE ACTUALLY WORKING.	A TRAVELER IS MAD THAT THEY CAN'T CARRY ON A SEDAN-SIZED DUFFEL BAG.
A TRAVELER MISTAKINGLY WAITS 1 HR IN A PRECHECK LINE—ONLY TO BE REJECTED.	MEMBERS OF A 'FUN' GROUP ARE ALL WEARING THE SAME SHIRT.	SOMEONE TAKES THEIR SHOES OFF WHILE ON THE PLANE.	THERE IS A 'SERVICE ANIMAL' THAT IS CLEARLY NOT A SERVICE ANIMAL.	THERE'S SIX GENERATIONS OF BIRDS LIVING IN THE RAFTERS.
A STRANGER SITS DOWN NEXT TO YOU DESPITE ALL THE OPEN SEATING.	A FAMILY OF THREE IS CARRYING ROUGHLY 23 SUITCASES.	EVERY SINGLE PERSON IN THE AIRPORT IS SEEMINGLY IN LINE FOR COFFEE.	PASSENGERS RUSH INTO THE AISLE THE MOMENT A FLIGHT LANDS.	THERE IS A CRYING BABY (OR ADULT).

OBJECTIVE

OH, YOU MEAN BESIDES TRYING TO PASS THE TIME DURING THIS VACATION THAT YOU MAY OR MAY NOT HAVE EVEN WANTED TO GO ON? ISN'T THAT ENOUGH? WHAT DO YOU WANT FROM US?

WELL, WE HOPE YOU'RE AT LEAST FAMILIAR WITH THE CONCEPT OF BINGO. BECAUSE IF NOT, WELL WE ARE REALLY KIND OF WORRIED ABOUT YOU. WHAT OTHER THINGS IN LIFE HAVE YOU MISSED? SHOES? AUTOMOBILES? TWO-PLY TOILET PAPER? WE DIGRESS.

THIS VACATION BIN·GO GAME IS PLAYED MUCH LIKE THE TRADITIONAL ONE. YOUR GOAL IS TO SIMPLY BE THE FIRST TO FILL 5 SEQUENTIAL SQUARES IN A ROW, A COLUMN, OR EVEN DIAGONALLY (SEE FIGURE 1 BELOW).

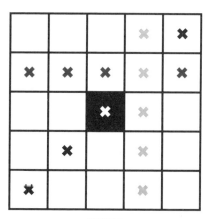

FIGURE 1

SEE THAT X IN THE CENTER SQUARE OF YOUR BOARDS? THAT'S A FREE SQUARE—WHICH MEANS EVERY PLAYER GETS THIS ONE AUTOMATICALLY. IT REALLY HELPS SO...YOU'RE WELCOME.

PLAYING THE GAME

AFTER DETERMINING HOW MANY PEOPLE ARE PLAYING, THE OWNER OF THE BOOK SHOULD PERF. OUT A CARD (OR TWO) FOR EVERYONE TO USE AS THEIR PLAY BOARD(S).

ALRIGHT, SO HERE'S HOW OUR GAME IS A BIT DIFFERENT. WE'VE PRE-FILLED EACH CARD WITH THE COMMON (YET RIDICULOUS) THINGS THAT ALWAYS SEEM TO HAPPEN WHILE TRAVELING. SO, INSTEAD OF SOMEONE JUST CALLING OUT NUMBERS, EVERYONE IS PEOPLE WATCHING INSTEAD. WHEN SOMETHING HAPPENS THAT IS ON ONE OF YOUR SQUARES, YOU CALL IT OUT (AS DISCREETLY AS APPROPRIATE, OF COURSE) AND MARK OFF THE SQUARE.

JUST REMEMBER THAT THE OTHER PLAYERS NEED TO BE AWARE OF THE 'CALL'—AND IDEALLY SEE IT AS WELL (BUT THAT'S NOT A REQUIREMENT). THAT WAY THEY CAN ALSO MARK OFF THAT SQUARE IF IT'S ON THEIR BOARD.

WINNING

WHEN A PLAYER MARKS OFF A WINNING CARD, THEY SHOULD ANNOUNCE 'BINGO.' IN THE EVENT OF A TIE, THE FIRST TO SAY IT IS THE WINNER. EITHER WAY—EVERYONE ELSE IN THE ROOM WILL PROBABLY BE WONDERING WHAT THE HELL YOU ARE DOING. ADMITTEDLY IT MIGHT BE HARD TO MAKE A TRUE BINGO, SO YOU CAN ALSO DECIDE THAT THE PLAYER WITH THE MOST SQUARES MARKED OFF IS THE WINNER.

BONUS: YOU CAN ALSO PLAY THIS AS A DRINKING GAME. IT'S SIMPLE. WHEN SOMETHING HAPPENS ON YOUR CARD, YOU HAVE TO TAKE A DRINK (AFTER TRAVELING IS DONE OF COURSE). IF YOU MAKE A BINGO—WELL NOW EVERYONE ELSE HAS TO DRINK. JUST TALLY UP DRINKS ONCE YOU'RE AT YOUR DESTINATION & GO TO THE BAR.

BIN×GO

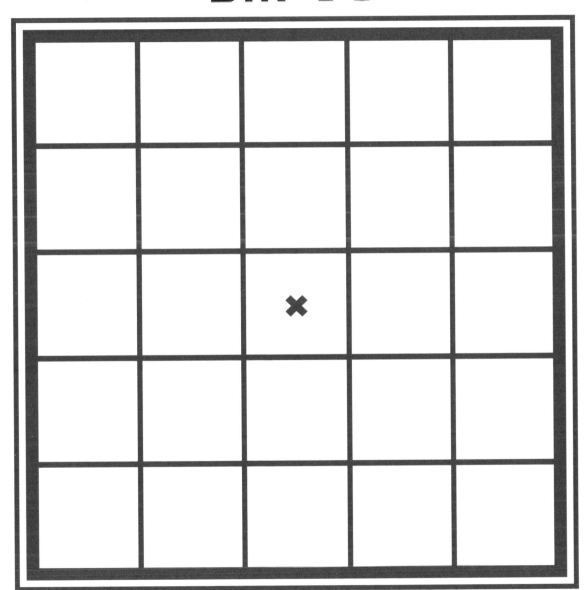

OBJECTIVE

THIS TIME, IT'S PERSONAL—LITERALLY. YOU KNOW YOUR FAMILY & FRIENDS BEST, SO USE THESE SIX CARDS TO CREATE YOUR OWN HIGHLY SPECIFIC BINGO GAME. DOES YOUR FRIEND JIMMY ALWAYS EAT BEEF JERKY BY THE TRUCK LOAD WHILE IN THE CAR? WELL, YOU SHOULD FILL A SQUARE WITH IT. CREATE A GAME FOR ROAD TRIPS, FAMILY VACATIONS, OR SOMETHING ELSE ENTIRELY. WE'LL LEAVE THAT UP TO YOU. YOU PURCHASED THIS BOOK AFTER ALL, IT'S THE LEAST WE COULD DO.

REGARDLESS, THIS BIN·GO GAME IS PLAYED MUCH LIKE THE TRADITIONAL ONE. YOUR GOAL IS TO SIMPLY BE THE FIRST TO FILL FIVE SEQUENTIAL SQUARES IN A ROW, A COLUMN, OR EVEN DIAGONALLY (SEE FIGURE 1 BELOW).

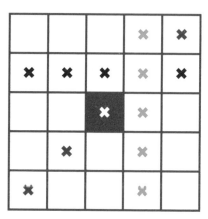

FIGURE 1

SEE THAT X IN THE CENTER SQUARE OF YOUR BOARDS? THAT'S A FREE SQUARE—WHICH MEANS EVERY PLAYER GETS THIS ONE AUTOMATICALLY. IT REALLY HELPS SO...YOU'RE WELCOME.

PLAYING THE GAME

AFTER DETERMINING HOW MANY PEOPLE ARE PLAYING, THE OWNER OF THE BOOK SHOULD PERF. OUT A CARD (OR TWO) FOR EVERYONE TO USE AS THEIR PLAY BOARD(S).

ALRIGHT, SO HERE'S HOW OUR GAME IS A BIT DIFFERENT. WE'VE PRE-FILLED EACH CARD WITH THE COMMON (YET RIDICULOUS) THINGS THAT ALWAYS SEEM TO HAPPEN WHILE TRAVELING. SO, INSTEAD OF SOMEONE JUST CALLING OUT NUMBERS, EVERYONE IS PEOPLE WATCHING INSTEAD. WHEN SOMETHING HAPPENS THAT IS ON ONE OF YOUR SQUARES, YOU CALL IT OUT (AS DISCREETLY AS APPROPRIATE, OF COURSE) AND MARK OFF THE SQUARE.

JUST REMEMBER THAT THE OTHER PLAYERS NEED TO BE AWARE OF THE 'CALL'—AND IDEALLY SEE IT AS WELL (BUT THAT'S NOT A REQUIREMENT). THAT WAY THEY CAN ALSO MARK OFF THAT SQUARE IF IT'S ON THEIR BOARD.

WINNING

WHEN A PLAYER MARKS OFF A WINNING CARD, THEY SHOULD ANNOUNCE 'BINGO.' IN THE EVENT OF A TIE, THE FIRST TO SAY IT IS THE WINNER. EITHER WAY—EVERYONE ELSE IN THE ROOM WILL PROBABLY BE WONDERING WHAT THE HELL YOU ARE DOING. ADMITTEDLY IT MIGHT BE HARD TO MAKE A TRUE BINGO, SO YOU CAN ALSO DECIDE THAT THE PLAYER WITH THE MOST SQUARES MARKED OFF IS THE WINNER.

BONUS: YOU CAN ALSO PLAY THIS AS A DRINKING GAME. IT'S SIMPLE. WHEN SOMETHING HAPPENS ON YOUR CARD, YOU HAVE TO TAKE A DRINK (AFTER ANY DRIVING IS DONE, OF COURSE). IF YOU MAKE A BINGO—WELL NOW EVERYONE ELSE HAS TO DRINK. JUST TALLY UP DRINKS ONCE YOU'RE AT YOUR DESTINATION & GO TO THE BAR.

BIN×GO

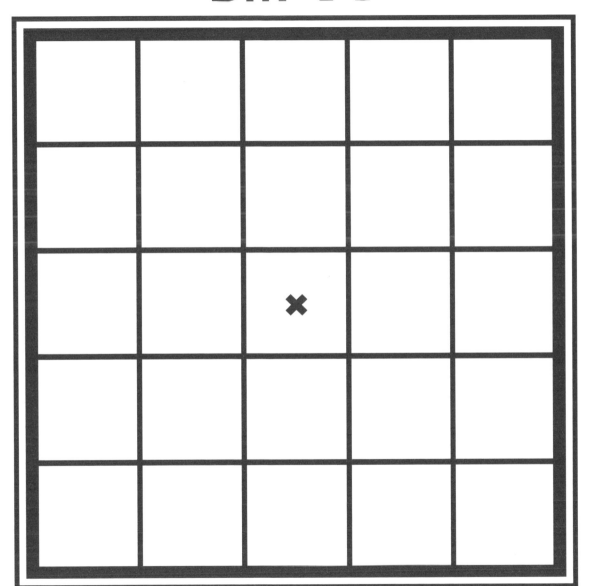

OBJECTIVE

THIS TIME, IT'S PERSONAL—LITERALLY. YOU KNOW YOUR FAMILY & FRIENDS BEST, SO USE THESE SIX CARDS TO CREATE YOUR OWN HIGHLY SPECIFIC BINGO GAME. DOES YOUR FRIEND JIMMY ALWAYS EAT BEEF JERKY BY THE TRUCK LOAD WHILE IN THE CAR? WELL, YOU SHOULD FILL A SQUARE WITH IT. CREATE A GAME FOR ROAD TRIPS, FAMILY VACATIONS, OR SOMETHING ELSE ENTIRELY. WE'LL LEAVE THAT UP TO YOU. YOU PURCHASED THIS BOOK AFTER ALL, IT'S THE LEAST WE COULD DO.

REGARDLESS, THIS BIN·GO GAME IS PLAYED MUCH LIKE THE TRADITIONAL ONE. YOUR GOAL IS TO SIMPLY BE THE FIRST TO FILL FIVE SEQUENTIAL SQUARES IN A ROW, A COLUMN, OR EVEN DIAGONALLY (SEE FIGURE 1 BELOW).

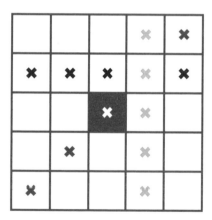

FIGURE 1

SEE THAT X IN THE CENTER SQUARE OF YOUR BOARDS? THAT'S A FREE SQUARE—WHICH MEANS EVERY PLAYER GETS THIS ONE AUTOMATICALLY. IT REALLY HELPS SO...YOU'RE WELCOME.

PLAYING THE GAME

AFTER DETERMINING HOW MANY PEOPLE ARE PLAYING, THE OWNER OF THE BOOK SHOULD PERF. OUT A CARD (OR TWO) FOR EVERYONE TO USE AS THEIR PLAY BOARD(S).

ALRIGHT, SO HERE'S HOW OUR GAME IS A BIT DIFFERENT. WE'VE PRE-FILLED EACH CARD WITH THE COMMON (YET RIDICULOUS) THINGS THAT ALWAYS SEEM TO HAPPEN WHILE TRAVELING. SO, INSTEAD OF SOMEONE JUST CALLING OUT NUMBERS, EVERYONE IS PEOPLE WATCHING INSTEAD. WHEN SOMETHING HAPPENS THAT IS ON ONE OF YOUR SQUARES, YOU CALL IT OUT (AS DISCREETLY AS APPROPRIATE, OF COURSE) AND MARK OFF THE SQUARE.

JUST REMEMBER THAT THE OTHER PLAYERS NEED TO BE AWARE OF THE 'CALL'—AND IDEALLY SEE IT AS WELL (BUT THAT'S NOT A REQUIREMENT). THAT WAY THEY CAN ALSO MARK OFF THAT SQUARE IF IT'S ON THEIR BOARD.

WINNING

WHEN A PLAYER MARKS OFF A WINNING CARD, THEY SHOULD ANNOUNCE 'BINGO.' IN THE EVENT OF A TIE, THE FIRST TO SAY IT IS THE WINNER. EITHER WAY—EVERYONE ELSE IN THE ROOM WILL PROBABLY BE WONDERING WHAT THE HELL YOU ARE DOING. ADMITTEDLY IT MIGHT BE HARD TO MAKE A TRUE BINGO, SO YOU CAN ALSO DECIDE THAT THE PLAYER WITH THE MOST SQUARES MARKED OFF IS THE WINNER.

BONUS: YOU CAN ALSO PLAY THIS AS A DRINKING GAME. IT'S SIMPLE. WHEN SOMETHING HAPPENS ON YOUR CARD, YOU HAVE TO TAKE A DRINK (AFTER ANY DRIVING IS DONE, OF COURSE). IF YOU MAKE A BINGO—WELL NOW EVERYONE ELSE HAS TO DRINK. JUST TALLY UP DRINKS ONCE YOU'RE AT YOUR DESTINATION & GO TO THE BAR.

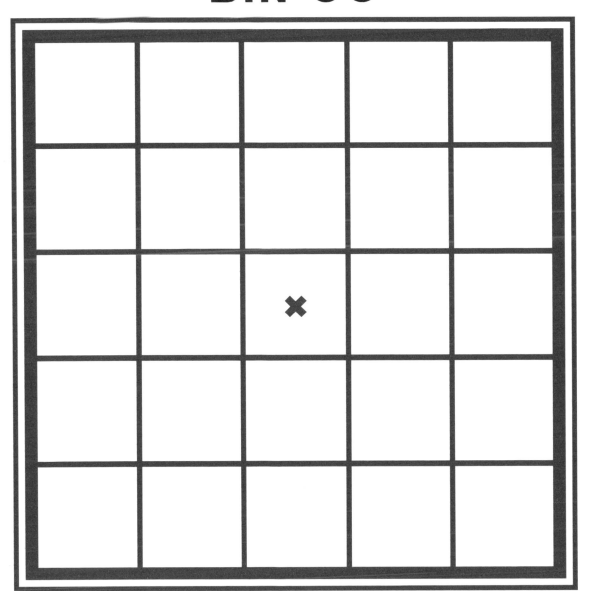

OBJECTIVE

THIS TIME, IT'S PERSONAL—LITERALLY. YOU KNOW YOUR FAMILY & FRIENDS BEST, SO USE THESE SIX CARDS TO CREATE YOUR OWN HIGHLY SPECIFIC BINGO GAME. DOES YOUR FRIEND JIMMY ALWAYS EAT BEEF JERKY BY THE TRUCK LOAD WHILE IN THE CAR? WELL, YOU SHOULD FILL A SQUARE WITH IT. CREATE A GAME FOR ROAD TRIPS, FAMILY VACATIONS, OR SOMETHING ELSE ENTIRELY. WE'LL LEAVE THAT UP TO YOU. YOU PURCHASED THIS BOOK AFTER ALL, IT'S THE LEAST WE COULD DO.

REGARDLESS, THIS BIN·GO GAME IS PLAYED MUCH LIKE THE TRADITIONAL ONE. YOUR GOAL IS TO SIMPLY BE THE FIRST TO FILL FIVE SEQUENTIAL SQUARES IN A ROW, A COLUMN, OR EVEN DIAGONALLY (SEE FIGURE 1 BELOW).

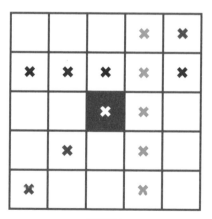

FIGURE 1

SEE THAT X IN THE CENTER SQUARE OF YOUR BOARDS? THAT'S A FREE SQUARE—WHICH MEANS EVERY PLAYER GETS THIS ONE AUTOMATICALLY. IT REALLY HELPS SO...YOU'RE WELCOME.

PLAYING THE GAME

AFTER DETERMINING HOW MANY PEOPLE ARE PLAYING, THE OWNER OF THE BOOK SHOULD PERF. OUT A CARD (OR TWO) FOR EVERYONE TO USE AS THEIR PLAY BOARD(S).

ALRIGHT, SO HERE'S HOW OUR GAME IS A BIT DIFFERENT. WE'VE PRE-FILLED EACH CARD WITH THE COMMON (YET RIDICULOUS) THINGS THAT ALWAYS SEEM TO HAPPEN WHILE TRAVELING. SO, INSTEAD OF SOMEONE JUST CALLING OUT NUMBERS, EVERYONE IS PEOPLE WATCHING INSTEAD. WHEN SOMETHING HAPPENS THAT IS ON ONE OF YOUR SQUARES, YOU CALL IT OUT (AS DISCREETLY AS APPROPRIATE, OF COURSE) AND MARK OFF THE SQUARE.

JUST REMEMBER THAT THE OTHER PLAYERS NEED TO BE AWARE OF THE 'CALL'—AND IDEALLY SEE IT AS WELL (BUT THAT'S NOT A REQUIREMENT). THAT WAY THEY CAN ALSO MARK OFF THAT SQUARE IF IT'S ON THEIR BOARD.

WINNING

WHEN A PLAYER MARKS OFF A WINNING CARD, THEY SHOULD ANNOUNCE 'BINGO.' IN THE EVENT OF A TIE, THE FIRST TO SAY IT IS THE WINNER. EITHER WAY—EVERYONE ELSE IN THE ROOM WILL PROBABLY BE WONDERING WHAT THE HELL YOU ARE DOING. ADMITTEDLY IT MIGHT BE HARD TO MAKE A TRUE BINGO, SO YOU CAN ALSO DECIDE THAT THE PLAYER WITH THE MOST SQUARES MARKED OFF IS THE WINNER.

BONUS: YOU CAN ALSO PLAY THIS AS A DRINKING GAME. IT'S SIMPLE. WHEN SOMETHING HAPPENS ON YOUR CARD, YOU HAVE TO TAKE A DRINK (AFTER ANY DRIVING IS DONE, OF COURSE). IF YOU MAKE A BINGO—WELL NOW EVERYONE ELSE HAS TO DRINK. JUST TALLY UP DRINKS ONCE YOU'RE AT YOUR DESTINATION & GO TO THE BAR.

BIN×GO

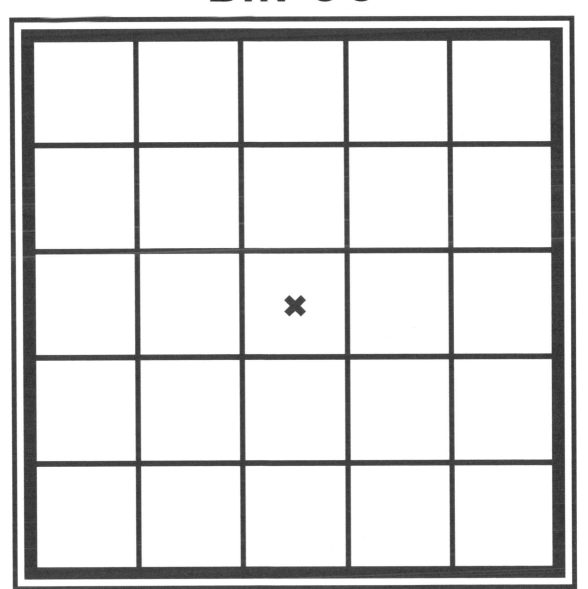

OBJECTIVE

THIS TIME, IT'S PERSONAL—LITERALLY. YOU KNOW YOUR FAMILY & FRIENDS BEST, SO USE THESE SIX CARDS TO CREATE YOUR OWN HIGHLY SPECIFIC BINGO GAME. DOES YOUR FRIEND JIMMY ALWAYS EAT BEEF JERKY BY THE TRUCK LOAD WHILE IN THE CAR? WELL, YOU SHOULD FILL A SQUARE WITH IT. CREATE A GAME FOR ROAD TRIPS, FAMILY VACATIONS, OR SOMETHING ELSE ENTIRELY. WE'LL LEAVE THAT UP TO YOU. YOU PURCHASED THIS BOOK AFTER ALL, IT'S THE LEAST WE COULD DO.

REGARDLESS, THIS BIN·GO GAME IS PLAYED MUCH LIKE THE TRADITIONAL ONE. YOUR GOAL IS TO SIMPLY BE THE FIRST TO FILL FIVE SEQUENTIAL SQUARES IN A ROW, A COLUMN, OR EVEN DIAGONALLY (SEE FIGURE 1 BELOW).

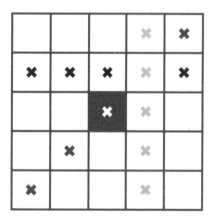

FIGURE 1

SEE THAT X IN THE CENTER SQUARE OF YOUR BOARDS? THAT'S A FREE SQUARE—WHICH MEANS EVERY PLAYER GETS THIS ONE AUTOMATICALLY. IT REALLY HELPS SO...YOU'RE WELCOME.

PLAYING THE GAME

AFTER DETERMINING HOW MANY PEOPLE ARE PLAYING, THE OWNER OF THE BOOK SHOULD PERF. OUT A CARD (OR TWO) FOR EVERYONE TO USE AS THEIR PLAY BOARD(S).

ALRIGHT, SO HERE'S HOW OUR GAME IS A BIT DIFFERENT. WE'VE PRE-FILLED EACH CARD WITH THE COMMON (YET RIDICULOUS) THINGS THAT ALWAYS SEEM TO HAPPEN WHILE TRAVELING. SO, INSTEAD OF SOMEONE JUST CALLING OUT NUMBERS, EVERYONE IS PEOPLE WATCHING INSTEAD. WHEN SOMETHING HAPPENS THAT IS ON ONE OF YOUR SQUARES, YOU CALL IT OUT (AS DISCREETLY AS APPROPRIATE, OF COURSE) AND MARK OFF THE SQUARE.

JUST REMEMBER THAT THE OTHER PLAYERS NEED TO BE AWARE OF THE 'CALL'—AND IDEALLY SEE IT AS WELL (BUT THAT'S NOT A REQUIREMENT). THAT WAY THEY CAN ALSO MARK OFF THAT SQUARE IF IT'S ON THEIR BOARD.

WINNING

WHEN A PLAYER MARKS OFF A WINNING CARD, THEY SHOULD ANNOUNCE 'BINGO.' IN THE EVENT OF A TIE, THE FIRST TO SAY IT IS THE WINNER. EITHER WAY—EVERYONE ELSE IN THE ROOM WILL PROBABLY BE WONDERING WHAT THE HELL YOU ARE DOING. ADMITTEDLY IT MIGHT BE HARD TO MAKE A TRUE BINGO, SO YOU CAN ALSO DECIDE THAT THE PLAYER WITH THE MOST SQUARES MARKED OFF IS THE WINNER.

BONUS: YOU CAN ALSO PLAY THIS AS A DRINKING GAME. IT'S SIMPLE. WHEN SOMETHING HAPPENS ON YOUR CARD, YOU HAVE TO TAKE A DRINK (AFTER ANY DRIVING IS DONE, OF COURSE). IF YOU MAKE A BINGO—WELL NOW EVERYONE ELSE HAS TO DRINK. JUST TALLY UP DRINKS ONCE YOU'RE AT YOUR DESTINATION & GO TO THE BAR.

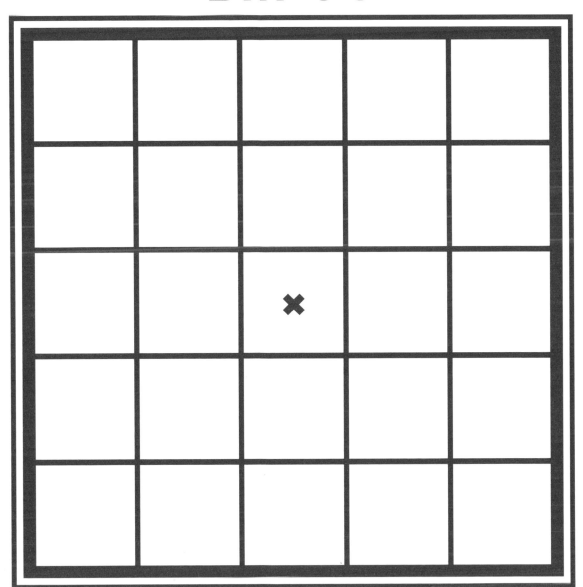

OBJECTIVE

THIS TIME, IT'S PERSONAL—LITERALLY. YOU KNOW YOUR FAMILY & FRIENDS BEST, SO USE THESE SIX CARDS TO CREATE YOUR OWN HIGHLY SPECIFIC BINGO GAME. DOES YOUR FRIEND JIMMY ALWAYS EAT BEEF JERKY BY THE TRUCK LOAD WHILE IN THE CAR? WELL, YOU SHOULD FILL A SQUARE WITH IT. CREATE A GAME FOR ROAD TRIPS, FAMILY VACATIONS, OR SOMETHING ELSE ENTIRELY. WE'LL LEAVE THAT UP TO YOU. YOU PURCHASED THIS BOOK AFTER ALL. IT'S THE LEAST WE COULD DO.

REGARDLESS, THIS BIN·GO GAME IS PLAYED MUCH LIKE THE TRADITIONAL ONE. YOUR GOAL IS TO SIMPLY BE THE FIRST TO FILL FIVE SEQUENTIAL SQUARES IN A ROW, A COLUMN, OR EVEN DIAGONALLY (SEE FIGURE 1 BELOW).

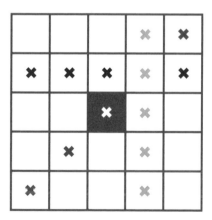

FIGURE 1

SEE THAT X IN THE CENTER SQUARE OF YOUR BOARDS? THAT'S A FREE SQUARE—WHICH MEANS EVERY PLAYER GETS THIS ONE AUTOMATICALLY. IT REALLY HELPS SO...YOU'RE WELCOME.

PLAYING THE GAME

AFTER DETERMINING HOW MANY PEOPLE ARE PLAYING, THE OWNER OF THE BOOK SHOULD PERF. OUT A CARD (OR TWO) FOR EVERYONE TO USE AS THEIR PLAY BOARD(S).

ALRIGHT, SO HERE'S HOW OUR GAME IS A BIT DIFFERENT. WE'VE PRE-FILLED EACH CARD WITH THE COMMON (YET RIDICULOUS) THINGS THAT ALWAYS SEEM TO HAPPEN WHILE TRAVELING. SO, INSTEAD OF SOMEONE JUST CALLING OUT NUMBERS, EVERYONE IS PEOPLE WATCHING INSTEAD. WHEN SOMETHING HAPPENS THAT IS ON ONE OF YOUR SQUARES, YOU CALL IT OUT (AS DISCREETLY AS APPROPRIATE, OF COURSE) AND MARK OFF THE SQUARE.

JUST REMEMBER THAT THE OTHER PLAYERS NEED TO BE AWARE OF THE 'CALL'—AND IDEALLY SEE IT AS WELL (BUT THAT'S NOT A REQUIREMENT). THAT WAY THEY CAN ALSO MARK OFF THAT SQUARE IF IT'S ON THEIR BOARD.

WINNING

WHEN A PLAYER MARKS OFF A WINNING CARD, THEY SHOULD ANNOUNCE 'BINGO.' IN THE EVENT OF A TIE, THE FIRST TO SAY IT IS THE WINNER. EITHER WAY—EVERYONE ELSE IN THE ROOM WILL PROBABLY BE WONDERING WHAT THE HELL YOU ARE DOING. ADMITTEDLY IT MIGHT BE HARD TO MAKE A TRUE BINGO, SO YOU CAN ALSO DECIDE THAT THE PLAYER WITH THE MOST SQUARES MARKED OFF IS THE WINNER.

BONUS: YOU CAN ALSO PLAY THIS AS A DRINKING GAME. IT'S SIMPLE. WHEN SOMETHING HAPPENS ON YOUR CARD, YOU HAVE TO TAKE A DRINK (AFTER ANY DRIVING IS DONE, OF COURSE). IF YOU MAKE A BINGO—WELL NOW EVERYONE ELSE HAS TO DRINK. JUST TALLY UP DRINKS ONCE YOU'RE AT YOUR DESTINATION & GO TO THE BAR.

PERSONALIZED BIN×GO PERSONALIZED

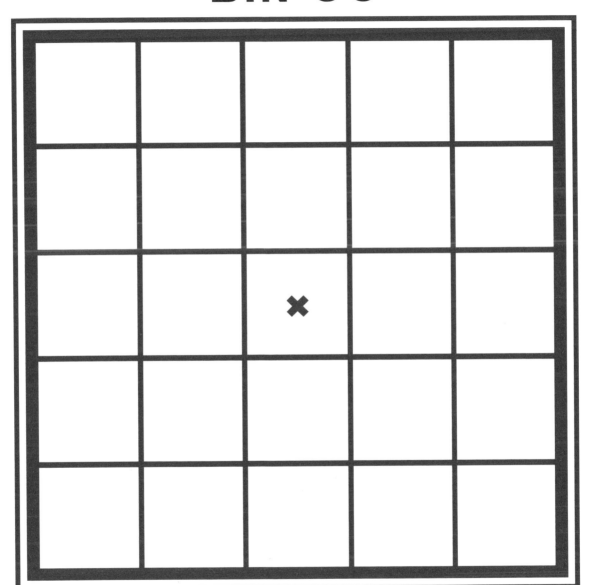

OBJECTIVE

THIS TIME, IT'S PERSONAL—LITERALLY. YOU KNOW YOUR FAMILY & FRIENDS BEST, SO USE THESE SIX CARDS TO CREATE YOUR OWN HIGHLY SPECIFIC BINGO GAME. DOES YOUR FRIEND JIMMY ALWAYS EAT BEEF JERKY BY THE TRUCK LOAD WHILE IN THE CAR? WELL, YOU SHOULD FILL A SQUARE WITH IT. CREATE A GAME FOR ROAD TRIPS, FAMILY VACATIONS, OR SOMETHING ELSE ENTIRELY. WE'LL LEAVE THAT UP TO YOU. YOU PURCHASED THIS BOOK AFTER ALL, IT'S THE LEAST WE COULD DO.

REGARDLESS, THIS BIN·GO GAME IS PLAYED MUCH LIKE THE TRADITIONAL ONE. YOUR GOAL IS TO SIMPLY BE THE FIRST TO FILL FIVE SEQUENTIAL SQUARES IN A ROW, A COLUMN, OR EVEN DIAGONALLY (SEE FIGURE 1 BELOW).

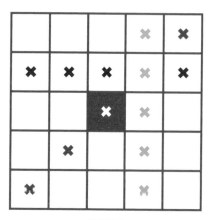

FIGURE 1

SEE THAT X IN THE CENTER SQUARE OF YOUR BOARDS? THAT'S A FREE SQUARE—WHICH MEANS EVERY PLAYER GETS THIS ONE AUTOMATICALLY. IT REALLY HELPS SO...YOU'RE WELCOME.

PLAYING THE GAME

AFTER DETERMINING HOW MANY PEOPLE ARE PLAYING, THE OWNER OF THE BOOK SHOULD PERF. OUT A CARD (OR TWO) FOR EVERYONE TO USE AS THEIR PLAY BOARD(S).

ALRIGHT, SO HERE'S HOW OUR GAME IS A BIT DIFFERENT. WE'VE PRE-FILLED EACH CARD WITH THE COMMON (YET RIDICULOUS) THINGS THAT ALWAYS SEEM TO HAPPEN WHILE TRAVELING. SO, INSTEAD OF SOMEONE JUST CALLING OUT NUMBERS, EVERYONE IS PEOPLE WATCHING INSTEAD. WHEN SOMETHING HAPPENS THAT IS ON ONE OF YOUR SQUARES, YOU CALL IT OUT (AS DISCREETLY AS APPROPRIATE, OF COURSE) AND MARK OFF THE SQUARE.

JUST REMEMBER THAT THE OTHER PLAYERS NEED TO BE AWARE OF THE 'CALL'—AND IDEALLY SEE IT AS WELL (BUT THAT'S NOT A REQUIREMENT). THAT WAY THEY CAN ALSO MARK OFF THAT SQUARE IF IT'S ON THEIR BOARD.

WINNING

WHEN A PLAYER MARKS OFF A WINNING CARD, THEY SHOULD ANNOUNCE 'BINGO.' IN THE EVENT OF A TIE, THE FIRST TO SAY IT IS THE WINNER. EITHER WAY—EVERYONE ELSE IN THE ROOM WILL PROBABLY BE WONDERING WHAT THE HELL YOU ARE DOING. ADMITTEDLY IT MIGHT BE HARD TO MAKE A TRUE BINGO, SO YOU CAN ALSO DECIDE THAT THE PLAYER WITH THE MOST SQUARES MARKED OFF IS THE WINNER.

BONUS: YOU CAN ALSO PLAY THIS AS A DRINKING GAME. IT'S SIMPLE. WHEN SOMETHING HAPPENS ON YOUR CARD, YOU HAVE TO TAKE A DRINK (AFTER ANY DRIVING IS DONE, OF COURSE). IF YOU MAKE A BINGO—WELL NOW EVERYONE ELSE HAS TO DRINK. JUST TALLY UP DRINKS ONCE YOU'RE AT YOUR DESTINATION & GO TO THE BAR.